THE RIME OF THE ANCIENT MARINER AND OTHER POEMS

By SAMUEL TAYLOR COLERIDGE

Introduction by JULIAN B. ABERNETHY

The Rime of the Ancient Mariner and Other Poems
By Samuel Taylor Coleridge
Introduction by Julian B. Abernethy

Print ISBN 13: 978-1-4209-5893-5
eBook ISBN 13: 978-1-4209-5894-2

This edition copyright © 2018. Digireads.com Publishing.

All rights reserved. No part of this publication may be reproduced, distributed, or transmitted in any form or by any means, including photocopying, recording, or other electronic or mechanical methods, without the prior written permission of the publisher, except in the case of brief quotations embodied in critical reviews and certain other noncommercial uses permitted by copyright law.

Cover Image: a detail of an illustration by A. C. Michael which appeared in "My Book of Stories from the Poets" by Christine Chaundler, published by Funk & Wagnalls company, New York, 1920.

Please visit *www.digireads.com*

CONTENTS

Introduction 5

The Rime of the Ancient Mariner 32

    Argument 32
    Part I 32
    Part II 35
    Part III 38
    Part IV 40
    Part V 43
    Part VI 47
    Part VII 50

Kubla Khan 54

Christabel 57

    Part I 58
    The Conclusion to Part I 65
    Part II 66
    The Conclusion to Part II 74

The Eolian Harp 75

Reflections on Having Left a Place of Retirement 76

This Lime-Tree Bower My Prison 78

Frost at Midnight 80

Fears in Solitude 82

The Nightingale 88

Dejection: An Ode 91

The Pains of Sleep 95

To William Wordsworth 96

Introduction

BIOGRAPHICAL SKETCH

At Ottery St. Mary, in beautiful Devonshire, Samuel Taylor Coleridge was born, October 21, 1772. The father, vicar of the parish and head master of the Free Grammar School, was an amiable eccentric, with some scholarly knowledge and much innocent pedantry; "a perfect Parson Adams," the poet says, "in learning, good-heartedness, absentness of mind, and excessive ignorance of the world." The mother was a good practical housewife, with a fine scorn for "your harpsichord ladies," and a strong ambition to have her sons become gentlemen. All told, there were thirteen children in the family, of whom the poet was the youngest. At three years of age he attended a dame's school and at six he entered his father's school, where he "soon outstripped" all of his age.

As a lad, Coleridge was precocious and strange, showing early symptoms of the illustrious infirmities of later years. He cared little for the ordinary sports of boys, and naturally was tormented by them into isolation. Reading and dreaming were his chief occupations and joys. "At six years of age," he says, "I remember to have read *Belisarius, Robinson Crusoe,* and *Philip Quarll;* and then I found the *Arabian Nights' Entertainments,* one tale of which made so deep an impression on me . . . that I was haunted by specters whenever I was in the dark. . . . My father found out the effect which these books had produced, and burned them. So I became a dreamer, and acquired an indisposition to all bodily activity . . . and before I was eight years old I was *a character.*"

In the boy's ninth year, the father died, and the next year the little dreamer was sent to the famous charity school, Christ's Hospital, in London, which became his home for nine years. In *Frost at Midnight,* he says:

> "I was reared
> In the great city, pent 'mid cloisters dim,
> And saw nought lovely but the sky and stars."

Among the seven hundred "blue-coat" boys the youthful exile found a sympathetic companion in Charles Lamb, who became his life-long friend. The imagination loves to picture these two frail boys, marked for immortal fame, wandering about the streets of London, as we to-day see the boys of Christ's, in that antique garb—a long, blue coat, reaching nearly to the heels and buttoned straight to the neck in front, with yellow stockings, low shoes, a white stock, and bare head.

Christ's was a school of stern experiences in those days, hard fare, hard lessons, and hard floggings being the law of the boys' daily life. But the headmaster, the Rev. James Boyer, in spite of his Rhadamanthine methods, instructed the boys thoroughly well in Latin and Greek, and in the elements of manliness. "Thank Heaven," says Coleridge, "I was flogged instead of being flattered."

No severity of discipline could keep the visionary boy out of that world of romance and ideality which he had early created for himself. Once he was rushing along the street swinging his arms as if swimming, and, happening to hit a stranger's pocket with his hand, he was seized as a thief. Upon explaining that he thought himself Leander swimming the Hellespont, the man gave him a subscription to a circulating library. This providential supply of reading he rapidly devoured, "running all risks in skulking out to get the two volumes which I was entitled to have daily." His vagaries were not always so happy in their final issue. At one time, thinking himself an infidel, to escape being a minister he planned to run away and become apprenticed to a shoemaker; but master Boyer intervened with his characteristic application of common sense. "So, sirrah, you are an infidel, are you? Then I'll flog your infidelity out of you," and a summary conversion was effected.

Coleridge's reading during these school years was prodigious not only in its quantity and variety, but also in its profundity. A brother came to London to study in the hospitals, and so he "became wild to be apprenticed to a surgeon," he says; "English, Latin, yea, Greek books of medicine read I incessantly." A Latin medical dictionary he learned "nearly by heart." But this interest soon gave way to "a rage for metaphysics," and he read deeply in the Neo-Platonists and Church Fathers. "At a very premature age, even before my fifteenth year, I had bewildered myself in metaphysics, and in theological controversy." For a time history, even poetry, had no interest for him. His greatest delight was to meet "any passenger, especially if he were dressed in black," with whom he could bring about a discussion of his favorite theme, "providence, foreknowledge, will, and fate." It was of Coleridge at about this time that Lamb's famous sketch portrait was drawn. "Come back into memory, like as thou wert in the day-spring of thy fancies, with hope like a fiery column before thee—the dark pillar not yet turned—Samuel Taylor Coleridge—Logician, Metaphysician, Bard!— How have I seen the casual passer through the cloisters stand still, entranced with admiration (while he weighed the disproportion between the *speech* and the *garb* of the young Mirandula), to hear thee unfold, in thy deep and sweet intonations, the mysteries of Jamblichus, or Plotinus (for even in those years thou waxedst not pale at such philosophic draughts), or reciting Homer in his Greek, or Pindar—

while the walls of the old Grey Friars re-echoed to the accents of the *inspired charity boy!*"

From "this preposterous pursuit" of metaphysics, as he afterwards called it, Coleridge was reconverted to the pursuit of beauty and things of the imagination through a rather surprising agency. He read the *Sonnets* of William Lisle Bowles and discovered a new heaven and a new earth in poetry. With "impetuous zeal," he labored to win other appreciative readers, and with his own pen made forty copies of the sonnets as presents for his friends. Four years later, Wordsworth made the same discovery, and kept his brother waiting on Westminster Bridge while he read the volume through. This modest little collection of twenty-one sonnets seems to-day innocent enough of any such moving power, and one wonders what would have been the effect if Coleridge had first come upon Cowper and Burns. What surprised and transported him in these sonnets was the revelation of poetic simplicity and sincerity, and love of natural beauty, qualities strangely different from the placid conventionalisms of eighteenth-century poetry; and so for the time being the pensive Bowles became to Coleridge "the god of my idolatry."

In 1791 Coleridge entered Jesus College, Cambridge. Of his university life few details have survived. He won a gold medal for a Sapphic Ode, and just missed success in a close contest for a prize scholarship. A fellow student described his reading as "desultory and capricious." His scholarship apparently made no real impression except through the remarkable conversational powers for which he was distinguished throughout his life. Students flocked to his rooms to hear him discourse upon the exciting political issues of the time, when he would recite "whole passages verbatim" from the latest political pamphlets. Near the end of his second year occurred the most conspicuous episode of which we have any knowledge. Suddenly he went up to London and enlisted in the King's Light Dragoons, under the name of Silas Tomkyn Comberbach (S.T.C.)—an appropriate name, he afterwards suggested, as he presented but a sorry appearance upon a horse's back. Four months of soldiering was quite enough, and he managed to reveal his situation to friends, who procured his release and return to the university. This singular freak he attributed to debts and disappointment in love, but the real explanation is found in a constitutional instability of purpose, a tendency to pursue the fresh suggestions of impulse, new schemes of alluring colors, *ignes fatui,* that led him a deplorable race with the stern realities of life. It is not surprising, therefore, that a few months after the military adventure he left the university altogether, decoyed by a new appeal to his restless and romantic temperament.

While visiting a friend in Oxford, he met Robert Southey, a young enthusiast like himself, filled with the radicalism and democracy of the

French Revolution. A friendship was at once established, a partnership tragedy was written, *The Fall of Robespierre,* which Coleridge published at Cambridge; and out of a kinship of ideals was swiftly evolved the Utopian scheme of Pantisocracy, a state of individual and social perfection which was to be realized in a sort of communal paradise, established on the banks of the Susquehanna. For a time Pantisocracy was made famous in university circles, especially through the eloquence of Coleridge, and other idealists were enlisted in the project; but the very material consideration of the money required to emigrate to America was finally reached, and upon this rock the beautiful scheme went to pieces; not, however, until Coleridge's university career had been wrecked.

Coleridge now entered upon practical life, with a most unpractical grasp upon its responsibilities. Pantisocracy with its rose-colored idealism and inherent elements of disaster, was symbolical of his management of all of life's material problems. He began with a course of lectures, in Bristol, upon the burning question of liberty, which he called *Consciones ad Populum.* In October, 1795, in Chatterton's church of St. Mary Redcliffe, he was married to Miss Sara Fricker, whose sister Edith, a month later, became the wife of his friend Southey. The young couple settled at Clevedon, in a "pretty cot," over which "thick jasmines twined," where they could hear—

"At silent noon, and eve, and early morn,
The sea's faint murmur."

The happiness of this first home is recorded in *The Eolian Harp* and *Reflections on having left a Place of Retirement.*

A generous publisher of Bristol, Joseph Cottle, offered Coleridge a guinea and a half for every hundred lines of poetry he would write. Upon this insubstantial vision of golden harvests as a basis, he set up his domestic establishment. In 1797 he published his first volume of poetry, entitled *Poems on Various Subjects,* including in the volume three sonnets by his friend Lamb. He started a weekly magazine, called *The Watchman,* which came to an impecunious end with the tenth number. Very soon he proved—to his friends, if not to himself—how precarious is literature as a trade to live by, especially when carried on by a genius. He wrote poems and book-reviews for the magazines, planned great works which came to nothing, preached in Unitarian chapels, but without pay; he received gifts and loans from friends; he took into his family as a boarder and pupil, Charles Lloyd, a wealthy young man of literary ambition, who became one of the "Lakers." But his finances became increasingly chaotic, and in deep distress he writes, "my anxieties eat me up."

A small cottage at Nether Stowey, provided by his friend, Thomas Poole, into which he moved in 1797, seemed to promise a happy remedy for all his ills. Here he will become a farmer, "and there can be no shadow of a doubt that an acre and a half of land, divided properly, and managed properly, will maintain a small family in everything but clothes and rent." He will give up meat and strong liquors, both of which are "perceptibly" injurious. "Sixteen shillings," he estimates, will "cover all the weekly expenses." To a friend who suggested the loneliness of so remote a place he replied: "I shall have six companions: my Sara, my babe, my own shaping and disquisitive mind, my books, my beloved friend, Thomas Poole, and lastly, Nature looking at me with a thousand looks of beauty, and speaking to me in a thousand melodies of love." And literature, "though I shall never abandon it, will always be a secondary object with me. My poetic vanity and my political *furor* have been exhaled; and I would rather be an expert, self-maintaining gardener than a Milton, if I could not unite both."

It is worth while to dwell at some length upon this bucolic dream, for in its fragmentary realization Coleridge came nearer to peace and happiness than was ever his fortune again. Soon after he was settled at Stowey, the most important event of his life occurred; at Racedown he met Wordsworth and his sister Dorothy, and mutual admiration ripened quickly into a friendship that linked together forever the names of these two poets. In a few weeks Wordsworth and his sister removed to Alfoxden, a pleasant country house near the sea, three miles from Stowey, their "principal inducement being," as Dorothy wrote, "Coleridge's society." For about a year the two poets were together almost daily; both were great walkers, and the Quantock hills echoed in all directions their high talk of poetry and the poetic art; and in those delightful rambles a new age of English poetry began. A literary partnership was formed and the epoch-making volume of *Lyrical Ballads* was published in September, 1798.

That Coleridge received more from this friendship than Wordsworth, there can be no doubt. From Wordsworth's lofty and steadfast purposes his emotional and receptive nature absorbed quickly the influence needed to stimulate and concentrate his best creative energies. Indeed, it is safe to say that without this influence Coleridge would have remained the second-rate poet of vagrant thought and voluminous expression found in his early writing. The year 1797–8, the period of this association, is called Coleridge's *annus mirabilis,* the wonderful year; for in this brief period he wrote essentially all the poetry upon which his fame as a poet rests, the *Ancient Mariner,* the first part of *Christabel,* the *Ode to France, Kubla Khan, Frost at Midnight, Fears in Solitude,* and *The Nightingale.*

About this time Coleridge received an annuity of £150 from the Wedgewood brothers, sons of the famous potter; the only condition of the gift was that he should devote himself entirely to the highest intellectual pursuits. With this bountiful providence to attend him, he set out for Germany, accompanied by Wordsworth and his sister. Nine months were devoted to the mastering of the German language, literature, and philosophy, a feat which, through his omnivorous powers of acquisition, he approximately accomplished. The most immediate result of this German excursion was a translation of Schiller's *Wallenstein,* of which Scott remarked: "Coleridge has made Schiller's *Wallenstein* far finer than he found it." Other results of these studies appeared later in the field of his philosophical speculations.

In the autumn of 1799, Coleridge and Wordsworth made a tour through the Lake Country, and in this visit the poetic fame of this region had its birth. They were especially charmed by the beauties of Grasmere, and here Wordsworth and his sister at once settled, in Dove Cottage, which to-day is a shrine of devoted pilgrimage. Six months later Coleridge found a home at Greta Hall, Keswick, twelve miles from Dove Cottage. The distance did not keep the friends apart long at a time, for to these peripatetic poets a brisk walk of twelve miles was only a stimulating exercise, when there was a reading and discussion of each other's poems in anticipation at the end. Interesting glimpses of these visits back and forth between Dove Cottage and Greta Hall, as between Stowey and Alfoxden, are given in Dorothy Wordsworth's faithful journals. In 1803 Southey with his family visited the Coleridges, and the visit was extended into a life-long residence. For ten years Greta Hall was nominally the home of Coleridge, and became permanently the home of his wife and children, who were finally left to the brotherly care of Southey.

The culmination of Coleridge's work as a poet was reached in 1802, when he published *Dejection: an Ode,* a pathetic confession of powers shattered and hopes unrealized. After this he wrote no more poetry of high merit. Henceforth, his life was a tragic decline, a losing fight against himself. The tragedies of life are the products of ignorance and weakness, but Nemesis accepts no excuses. Coleridge was not ignorant, and the knowledge of his weakness increased his suffering, while he paid the penalty of accumulated errors. He complains of the "God Pecunia," who compels him to write political articles for the *Morning Post*—Pegasus in the harness of a newspaper hack. But other and greater powers of evil than poverty were devastating his life. The demon of ill health was his familiar companion, in league always with the demon of procrastination, furnishing plausible excuses for wasted time and evaded obligations. The unsympathetic Hazlitt said that "Coleridge was capable of doing anything which did not present itself as a duty." There was also the demon of domestic infelicity. His marriage was hasty and proved to be "most ill-starred." But possibly there could be only incompatibility between a practical-minded wife, devoted to her children, and a husband disposed to substitute philosophical speculations for the substantial necessities of the household. He complained that she did not understand his philosophy, and she complained that he did not understand his duty to his children, and both were right. The solution was characteristic of his calamitous weakness; in 1810 he abandoned his home altogether.

There was another demon greater than all that presided over the majestic ruin of Coleridge's life, the demon of opium. From an early period he was a frequent sufferer from rheumatism, neuralgia, gout, and other ailments, partly inherited from the recklessness of youth. In 1797 he speaks of taking an opiate to alleviate pain, and by the year 1803 the opium habit had become established as a dissipation. In 1826, when he had measurably subdued the fiend, he wrote: "Alas! it is with a bitter smile, a laugh of gall and bitterness, that I recall this period of unsuspecting delusion, and how I first became aware of the maelstrom, the fatal whirlpool to which I was drawing, just when the current was beyond my strength to stem." De Quincey asserts, rather too positively, that opium "killed Coleridge as a poet." Certain it is that under its influence his poetic imagination seemed to be paralyzed, and an interest in metaphysical studies almost entirely supplanted the old poetic enthusiasm.

In 1804 Coleridge went to Malta for his health, and in about two years returned, "ill, penniless, and worse than homeless," he wrote to Wedgewood. He contributed to the London papers; started another magazine called *The Friend*, which failed like *The Watchman;* gave lectures upon Shakspere, the fragmentary notes and reports of which have made him famous as a critic; completed a tragedy, *Remorse,* which through the aid of Byron was accepted and successfully acted at Drury Lane Theater. In 1816 he published *Christabel,* which had long been lying in manuscript, and the next year he published the chief collection of his poems under the title *Sibylline Leaves,* "in allusion," he says, "to the fragmentary and wildly scattered state in which they had been long suffered to remain." During these years, 1804-1816, he was never long in one place, dodging in and out of London, appearing suddenly at one friend's house and then at another's, where a flying visit would often be prolonged into a residence of weeks or months. Naturally, he was always in financial distress, and his strenuous borrowing from friends in any but a poet and philosopher would be regarded as little better than begging. Old friends gradually fell away, through exhausted forbearance, but there were always new ones to pull him out of trouble. New acquaintances he impressed as the ideal genius, sadly unfortunate, frail of will and irresponsible, it might be, but brilliant and fascinating; so homes and hearts were readily opened to him. His active mind was constantly evolving great literary and philosophical projects that were never carried beyond the title page, such as this: "Logosophia, or On the Logos, Human and Divine, in Six Treatises." Publishers even sometimes advanced money on these mythical works. As early as his trip to Germany, he said accurately of his "waverings" of mind: "This is the disease of my mind—it is comprehensive in its conceptions and wastes itself in the contemplation of the many things which it might do." This "disease" had now been so increased by opium that his mind was capable of little else than metaphysical meanderings.

In 1816 Coleridge took heroic measures to overcome the opium habit, under which both health and mind were giving way. He put himself in the hands of a physician, and arranged for systematic treatment in the home of Mr. Gillman, at High-gate, just outside of London. Here he spent the remaining years of his life, in comparative peace and happiness. Under the patient and loving care of Mr. and Mrs. Gillman, whom he described in his will as "his more than friends, the guardians of his health, happiness, and interests," he recovered in large measure from the effects of the "detested poison," and renewed with more system and efficiency his literary activity. He now published his most important prose works, the *Aids to Reflection,* a book of religious meditations that was once widely popular, and the *Biographia Literaria,* a work containing little biography, but much and important literary criticism, profound in the analysis and exposition of poetic principles. This book and the *Table Talk,* notes of conversations written down by his nephew and son-in-law, Henry Nelson Coleridge, are the only prose works of Coleridge that attract readers to-day.

During these last years, Coleridge wrote little poetry, but one fragment, composed in 1827 and entitled, *Work without Hope,* is of peculiar interest, being perhaps the saddest lines a poet ever wrote of himself. He contrasts the spring, awakening to new life and productive energy, with his own dead and decaying powers:

> ALL Nature seems at work. Slugs leave their lair—
> The bees are stirring—birds are on the wing—
> And WINTER, slumbering in the open air,
> Wears on his smiling face a dream of Spring!
> And I, the while, the sole unbusy thing,
> Nor honey make, nor pair, nor build, nor sing.

Yet well I ken the banks where Amaranths blow,
Have traced the fount whence streams of nectar flow.
Bloom, O ye Amaranths! bloom for whom ye may,
For me ye bloom not! Glide, rich streams away!
With lips unbrightened, wreathless brow, I stroll:
And would you learn the spells that drowse my soul?
WORK WITHOUT HOPE draws nectar in a sieve,
And HOPE without an object cannot live.

Coleridge died in 1834, and the body that had done him such "grievous wrong" was laid in Highgate Churchyard. Few even of his admiring friends understood how great a light had gone out. When the news reached Wordsworth, he was deeply moved and spoke of Coleridge as "the most *wonderful* man that he had ever known." "His great and dear spirit haunts me," wrote Charles Lamb; "never saw I his likeness, nor probably the world can see again." There were three surviving children. Hartley, the oldest son, was a poet and essayist, gentle, lovable, and talented, but deprived of high achievement by intemperance. He spent his life in the Lake Country, near to Wordsworth, where his father had predicted he would "wander like a breeze." Derwent was a teacher, rector, and linguist, possessing something of his father's brilliant conversational gift. His daughter, Sarah, was distinguished for her intellectual acquirements, as well as for beauty and grace of personality. Her fine qualities are affectionately celebrated by Wordsworth in *The Triad.*

Coleridge's personal appearance has been described by many of his friends and contemporaries. The description of him by Dorothy Wordsworth at he was in the Stowey days is among the most celebrated of the word portraits. "He is a wonderful man," she writes in her journal. "His conversation teems with soul, mind, and spirit. Then he is so benevolent, so good-tempered and cheerful, and, like William, interests himself so much about every little trifle. At first I thought him very plain, that is for about three minutes; he is pale, thin, has a wide mouth, thick lip, and not very good teeth, longish, loose-growing, half-curling, rough-black hair. But if you hear him speak for five minutes, you think no more of them. His eye is large and full, and not very dark, but grey—such an eye as would receive from a heavy soul the dullest expression; but it speaks every emotion of his animated mind; it has more of 'the poet's eye in a fine frenzy rolling' than I ever witnessed. He has fine dark eyebrows, and an overhanging forehead."

His appearance in the last days at Highgate is given in Carlyle's powerfully drawn sketch: "The good man, he was now getting old, towards sixty perhaps; and gave you the idea of a life that had been full of sufferings; a life heavy-laden, half-vanquished, still swimming painfully in seas of manifold physical and other bewilderment. Brow and head were round, and of massive weight, but the face was flabby and irresolute. The deep eyes, of a light hazel, were as full of sorrow as of inspiration; confused pain looked wildly from them, as in a kind of mild astonishment. The whole figure and air, good and amiable otherwise, might be called flabby and irresolute; expressive of weakness under possibility of strength. He hung loosely on his limbs, with knees bent, and stooping attitude; in walking he rather shuffled than decisively stepped; and a lady once remarked, he never could fix which side of the garden-walk would suit him best, but continually shifted in cork-screw fashion, and kept trying both. A heavy-laden, high-aspiring and surely much-suffering man."

The character of Coleridge is easily misinterpreted, if the external facts of his personal history alone are considered. His great spirit, in spite of its incumbrances, was one of the strongest purifying and elevating influences of the nineteenth century. The clear stream of his poetry testifies to the crystal purity of the fountain head. Through noble sentiments, rational criticism, and the lofty reach of his philosophical thought he influenced and guided the finest minds of the century. He was the father of modern Shaksperian study, and laid the broad basis of modern criticism through sympathetic interpretation. He introduced German literature and philosophy into England, and sowed the seeds of transcendentalism, gathered from Kant and Schelling, which came to blossom and fruitage in the writings of Emerson. His *Aids to Reflection* and other religious and theological writings led to the Broad Church movement with which Frederick Maurice and Dean Stanley were identified. His poetry was a direct creative force; of the Romantic School he may justly be regarded as the founder; the fragmentary *Christabel,* which was read, recited, and admired some years before publication, was the model followed by Scott and Byron in their famous metrical romances and tales. The Preraphael movement of Rossetti and his friends of the "Brotherhood," which Theodore Watts-Dunton has defined as "the renaissance of the spirit of wonder in poetry and art," was indebted directly to Coleridge for much of its initial impulse. Such briefly is the summary of the achievements of Coleridge as poet, critic, and "subtle-souled psychologist."

COLERIDGE AS A TALKER

Among his contemporaries, Coleridge's chief influence was exerted through his marvelous conversational power. "He distinguished himself," says Carlyle, "to all that ever heard him as the most surprising talker extant in this world." Through this perishable form of expression he loved best, and was best able fully, to translate himself. "I think, Charles, you never heard me preach," he once remarked to

Lamb, who replied, "I never heard you do anything else." His lectures, according to all accounts, differed little from his ordinary talks, except in the number of the audiences. Highgate became famous as a resort for the eager-minded young men of the period, who listened reverently to the great sage's discourse, like disciples at the feet of a prophet. Among the more casual visitors was Emerson, who found the visit to be "rather a spectacle than a conversation." Upon the mention of Dr. Channing's name, "he burst into a declamation upon the folly and ignorance of Unitarianism." When, during a pause for breath, Emerson interposed that he himself had been born and bred a Unitarian, Coleridge replied, "'Yes, I supposed so,' and continued as before."

Of those who visited Highgate, Carlyle has left the most celebrated account of what was experienced there. "Coleridge sat on the brow of Highgate Hill, in those years, looking down on London and its smoke-tumult, like a sage escaped from the inanity of life's battle; attracting towards him the thoughts of innumerable brave souls still engaged there. His express contributions to poetry, philosophy, or any specific province of human literature or enlightenment, had been small and sadly intermittent; hut he had, especially among young inquiring men, a higher than literary, a kind of prophetic or magician character. He was thought to hold, he alone in England, the key of German and other Transcendentalisms; knew the sublime secret of believing by 'the reason' what 'the understanding' had been obliged to fling out as incredible. ... A sublime man; who, alone in those dark days, had saved his crown of spiritual manhood; escaping from the black materialisms, and revolutionary deluges, with 'God, Freedom, Immortality' still his: a king of men. The practical intellects of the world did not much heed him, or carelessly reckoned him a metaphysical dreamer; but to the rising spirits of the young generation he had this dusky sublime character; and sat there as a kind of *Magus,* girt in mystery and enigma. . . . Nothing could be more copious than his talk; and furthermore it was always, virtually or literally, of the nature of a monologue; suffering no interruption, however reverent; hastily putting aside all foreign additions, annotations, or most ingenuous desires for elucidation, as well-meant superfluities which would never do. Besides, it was talk not flowing any whither like a river, but spreading every whither in inextricable currents and regurgitations like a lake or sea; terribly deficient in definite goal or aim, nay often in logical intelligibility; *what* you were to believe or do, on any earthly or heavenly thing, obstinately refusing to appear from it. So that, most times, you felt logically lost; swamped near to drowning in this tide of ingenious vocables, spreading out boundless as if to submerge the world."

John Sterling thus describes his first interview with Coleridge: "I was in his company about three hours; and of that time he spoke during two and three quarters. It would have been delightful to listen as attentively, and certainly easy for him to speak just as well, for the next forty-eight hours. On the whole, his conversation, or rather monologue, is by far the most interesting I ever heard or heard of. Dr. Johnson's talk, with which it is obvious to compare it, seems to me immeasurably inferior."

Charles Lamb gives a striking instance of Coleridge's power: "I dined yesterday in Parnassus, with Wordsworth, Coleridge, Rogers, and Tom Moore—half the poetry of England constellated and clustered in Gloucester Place! It was a delightful evening! Coleridge was in his finest vein of talk—had all the talk; and let 'em talk as they will of the envy of poets, I am sure not one there but was content to be nothing but a listener. The Muses were dumb while Apollo lectured."

COLERIDGE AS A POET

"His best work is but little, but of its kind it is perfect and unique. For exquisite metrical movement and for imaginative fantasy, there is nothing in our language to be compared with *Christabel,* and *Kubla Khan,* and the *Ancient Mariner.* The little poem called *Love* is not so good, but it touches with great grace that with which all sympathize. All that he did excellently might be bound up in twenty pages, but it should be bound in pure gold."—*Stopford Brooke's Primer of English Literature.*

"Coleridge is the great Musician of the romantic school of English poetry. His practice is the exact antithesis of Wordsworth's theory that there is no essential difference between the language of poetry and the language of prose. In him metrical movement is all in all. He was the first to depart from the lofty severe iambic movement which had satisfied the feeling of the eighteenth century, and, by associating picturesque images and antique phrases in melodious and flowing meters, to set the imagination free in a world quite removed from actual experience. His invention exercised a profound influence upon the course of English verse-composition."—*Courthope's Liberal Movement in English Literature.*

"Even in the dilapidation of his powers, due chiefly, if you will, to his own unthrifty management of them, we might, making proper deductions, apply to him what Mark Antony says of the dead Cæsar:

> 'He was the ruins of the noblest man
> That ever lived in the tide of time.'

Samuel Taylor Coleridge

Whatever may have been his faults and weaknesses, he was the man of all his generation to whom we should most unhesitatingly allow the distinction of genius, that is, of one authentically possessed from time to time by some influence that made him better and greater than himself. If he lost himself too much in what Mr. Pater has admirably called 'impassioned contemplation,' he has at least left us such a legacy as only genius, and genius not always, can leave."—*James Russell Lowell's Literary and Political Addresses.*

"Coleridge is conspicuous, to a degree beyond any other writer between Spenser and Rossetti, for a delicate, voluptuous languor, a rich melancholy, and a pitying absorption without vanity in his own conditions and frailties, carried so far that the natural objects of his verse take the qualities of the human Coleridge upon themselves. In Wordsworth we find a purer, loftier note, a species of philosophical severity which is almost stoic, a freshness of atmosphere which contrasts with Coleridge's opaline dream-haze, magnifying and distorting common things. Truth, sometimes pursued to the confines or past the confines of triviality, is Wordsworth's first object, and he never stoops to self-pity, rarely to self-study. Each of these marvelous poets is pre-eminently master of the phrase that charms and intoxicates, the sequence of simple words so perfect that it seems at once inevitable and miraculous. Yet here also a very distinct difference may be defined between the charm of Wordsworth and the magic of Coleridge. The former is held more under the author's control than the latter, and is less impulsive. It owes its impressiveness to a species of lofty candor which kindles at the discovery of some beautiful truth not seen before, and gives the full intensity of passion to its expression. The latter is a sort of Eolian harp (such as that with which he enlivened the street of Nether Stowey) over which the winds of emotion play, leaving the instrument often without a sound, or with none but broken murmurs, yet sometimes dashing from its chords a melody, vague and transitory indeed, but of a most unearthly sweetness. Wordsworth was not a great metrist; he essayed comparatively few and easy forms, and succeeded best when he was at his simplest. Coleridge, on the other hand, was an innovator; his *Christabel* revolutionized English prosody and opened the door to a thousand experiments; in *Kubla Khan* and in some of the lyrics, Coleridge attained a splendor of verbal melody which places him near the summit of the English Parnassus."—*Edmund Gosse's Modern English Literature.*

THE ANCIENT MARINER

Modern English poetry dates from the *Lyrical Ballads,* written in partnership by Wordsworth and Coleridge and published by Joseph Cottle, at Bristol, 1798. The young poets had been caught in the first whirlwind of the French Revolution, but had regained their footing, and now inaugurated a revolution in poetry. The little volume was as strange and radical a document as the new constitution of France. It was intended to be a protest against the mechanical and lifeless forms and stilted sentiments of eighteenth-century poetry, and an exposition of new sources of poetic truth and of more natural forms of expression. These purposes were explained in a brief preface, contributed by Wordsworth, which in an expanded form in subsequent editions became the basis of modern poetic criticism?

Two literary tendencies were prominent in the latter part of the eighteenth century, the return to nature for the inspiration and material of poetry, as in Cowper and Burns, and the revival of romanticism. Naturalism was already showing signs of weakness in becoming too natural, as in the dull matter-of-factness of Crabbe's poems; and romanticism was running into the wildest extravagance and absurdity in such tales as Walpole's *Castle of Otranto,* Mrs. Radcliffe's *Mysteries of Udolpho,* and "Monk" Lewis's *Tales of Terror and Wonder.* Naturalism was in need of more imagination, and romanticism was in need of more truth, In prose Scott rescued the romance from ruin, and in poetry it was the work of Wordsworth and Coleridge, begun in the *Lyrical Ballads,* to give sanity and permanent power to both tendencies.

Fortunately we have an account of the origin of this adventurous little volume from each of the poets. Wordsworth tells the story as follows:

"In the autumn of 1797, Mr. Coleridge, my sister, and myself started from Alfoxden pretty late in the afternoon with a view to visit Linton and the Valley of Stones near to it; and as our united funds were very small, we agreed to defray the expense of the tour by writing a poem to be sent to the *New Monthly Magazine.* Accordingly, we set off, and proceeded along the Quantock Hills towards Watchet; and in the course of this walk was planned the poem of the 'Ancient Mariner,' founded on a dream, as Mr. Coleridge said, of his friend Mr. Cruikshank. Much the greatest part of the story was Mr. Coleridge's invention, but certain parts I suggested; for example, some crime was to be committed which should bring upon the Old Navigator, as Coleridge afterwards delighted to call him, the spectral persecution, as a consequence of that crime and his own wanderings. I had been reading in Shelvocke's 'Voyages,' a day or two before, that while doubling

Cape Horn, they frequently saw albatrosses in that latitude, the largest sort of sea fowl, some extending their wings twelve or thirteen feet. 'Suppose,' said I, 'you represent him as having killed one of these birds on entering the South Sea, and that the tutelary spirits of these regions take upon them to avenge the crime.' The incident was thought fit for the purpose, and adopted accordingly. I also suggested the navigation of the ship by the dead men, but do not recollect that I had anything more to do with the scheme of the poem. The gloss with which it was subesquently accompanied was not thought of by either of us at the time, at least, not a hint of it was given to me, and I have no doubt it was a gratuitous afterthought. We began the composition together on that, to me, memorable evening. I furnished two or three lines at the beginning of the poem, in particular

> 'And listened like a three years' child:
> The Mariner had his will.'

These trifling contributions, all but one, which Mr. C. has with unnecessary scrupulosity recorded, slipped out of his mind, as they well might. As we endeavored to proceed conjointly (I speak of the same evening), our respective manners proved so widely different that it would have been quite presumptuous in me to do anything but separate from an undertaking upon which I could only have been a clog. . . . The 'Ancient Manner' grew and grew till it became too important for our first object, which was limited to our expectation of five pounds; and we began to think of a volume which was to consist, as Mr. Coleridge has told the world, of poems chiefly on supernatural subjects, taken from common life, but looked at, as much as might be, through an imaginative medium."

Coleridge's account is given in Chapter XIV of the *Biographia Literaria* as follows:

"During the first year that Mr. Wordsworth and I were neighbors, our conversations turned frequently on the two cardinal points of poetry, the power of exciting the sympathy of the reader by a faithful adherence to the truth of nature, and the power of giving the interest of novelty by the modifying colors of imagination. The sudden charm which accidents of light and shade, which moonlight or sunset diffused over a known and familiar landscape, appeared to represent the practicability of combining both. These are the poetry of nature. The thought suggested itself (to which of us I do not recollect) that a series of poems might be composed of two sorts. In the one, the incidents and agents were to be, in part at least, supernatural; and the excellence aimed at was to consist in the interesting of the affections by the dramatic truth of such emotions as would naturally accompany such situations, supposing them real. And real in this sense they have been to every human being who, from whatever source of delusion, has at any time believed himself under supernatural agency. For the second class, subjects were to be chosen from ordinary life; the characters and incidents were to be such as will be found in every village and its vicinity where there is a meditative and feeling mind to seek after them, or to notice them when they present themselves.

"In this idea originated the plan of the *Lyrical Ballads,* in which it was agreed that my endeavors should be directed to persons and characters supernatural, or at least romantic; yet so as to transfer from our inward nature a human interest and a semblance of truth sufficient to procure for these shadows of imagination that willing suspension of disbelief for the moment, which constitutes poetic faith. Mr. Wordsworth, on the other hand, was to propose to himself as his object, to give the charm of novelty to things of every day, and to excite a feeling analogous to the supernatural, by awakening the mind's attention from the lethargy of custom, and directing it to the loveliness and the wonders of the world before us; an inexhaustible treasure, but for which, in consequence of the film of familiarity and selfish solicitate, we have eyes, yet see not, ears that hear not, and hearts that neither feel nor understand.

"With this view I wrote the *Ancient Mariner,* and was preparing, among other poems, the *Dark Ladie,* and the *Christabel,* in which I should have more nearly realized my ideal than I had done in my first attempt. But Mr. Wordsworth's industry had proved so much more successful, and the number of his poems so much greater, that my compositions, instead of forming a balance, appeared rather an interpolation of heterogeneous matter. Mr. Wordsworth added two or three poems written in his own character, in the impassioned, lofty, and sustained diction which is characteristic of his genius. In this form the *Lyrical Ballads* were published."

The volume contained twenty-three poems, nineteen of them written by Wordsworth. The four contributed by Coleridge were the *Ancient Mariner, The Foster-Mother's Tale, The Nightingale: a Conversational Poem,* and *The Dungeon.* Among Wordsworth's poems were illustrations of his best and his worst work. There were the *Lines Written Above Tintern Abbey, We are Seven, Expostulation and Reply,* and *The Tables Turned;* but there were also *Goody Blake* and *The Idiot Boy,* which furnished a deal of merriment for the critics. The volume opened with the *Ancient Mariner* and closed with *Tintern Abbey.* The publication was anonymous, with nothing to indicate that there were two authors. Before the book issued from the press the poets had set out for Germany, and they heard nothing of its fortune with the public for several months, except the cheering news from Mrs. Coleridge that "the *Lyrical Ballads* are not liked at all by any."

The text of the *Ancient Mariner* was much changed by Coleridge in successive editions, portions being omitted and many passages being rewritten. The original title of the poem was *The Rime of the Ancyent Marinere, in Seven Parts.* The feature of extreme archaism in words and phrases was over-done at first, and was modified throughout the poem, in the second edition of the *Lyrical Ballads,* 1800. The title was changed to *The Ancient Mariner, A Poet's Reverie.* The "Argument" was rewritten as follows:

"How a Ship having first sailed to the Equator, was driven by Storms to the cold Country towards the South Pole; how the Ancient Mariner, cruelly, and in contempt of the laws of hospitality, killed a Sea-bird; and how he was followed by many strange Judgments; and in what manner he came back to his own Country."

In the next two editions of the *Lyrical Ballads,* 1802 and 1805, the Argument was omitted. It appeared again in *Sibylline Leaves,* the edition of 1817, together with more changes in the text, the addition of the marginal gloss, and the motto from Burnet. These repeated alterations may suggest the poet's unstable mind, but in general they show a refinement and ripening of critical judgment. Many changes of the text are given in the notes of this edition as illustrations of improvements.

In response to the demand for "sources" of the poet's material, minute research has discovered a few hints, in addition to those mentioned by Wordsworth, which he may possibly have utilized. A quaint narrative published in 1633, Captain Thomas James's *Strange and Dangerous Voyage . . . in his intended Discovery of the Northwest Passage into the South Sea,* has some claim to honors of this kind. The extent of Coleridge's possible indebtedness to this book is shown in the notes. The idea of the angelic navigation of the ship is thought to have been suggested by a story of a shipwreck in the "Letter of Saint Paulinus to Macarius," found in La Bigne's *Magna Bibliotheca Veterum Patrum,* 1618, in which an old man is the sole survivor of the ship's crew and the ship is navigated by "a crew of angels," and steered by the "Pilot of the World." It is quite possible that Coleridge had seen these strange narratives, for about that time he was "literary cormorant," he says, "deep in all out of the way books whether of the monkish times, or of the puritanical era." But all such remote hints do not affect the originality of the poem—of the poetry of the poem; they merely show how genius always assimilates crude material and reproduces it in forms of beautiful art.

Ingenious and somewhat perverse efforts have been made to find in the *Ancient Mariner* some deep moral or subtle symbolical meaning. Some think they see in it an allegory, shadowing forth "the terrible discipline of culture, through which man must pass in order to reach self-consciousness and self-determination." An illustration of this method of interpretation may be found in the *Journal of Speculative Philosophy,* Vol. 14. But the matter is made clear enough by the statement of the simple moral at the end, and if this will not satisfy the searcher after profundity, we have Coleridge's own words for it that no deeper moral was intended. In *Table Talk* he says:

"Mrs. Barbauld once told me that she admired the *Ancient Mariner* very much, but that there were two faults in it,—it was improbable, and had no moral. As for the probability, I owned that that might admit some question; but as to the want of a moral, I told her that in my own judgment the poem had too much; and that the only, or chief, fault, if I might say so, was the obtrusion of the moral sentiment so openly on the reader as a principle or cause of action in a work of such pure imagination. It ought to have had no more moral than the *Arabian Nights* tale of the merchant's sitting down to eat dates by the side of a well, and throwing the shells aside, and lo! a genie starts up, and says he *must* kill the aforesaid merchant *because* one of the date-shells had, it seems, put out the eye of the genie's son."

The form of the *Ancient Mariner* is that of the ballad. Wordsworth says in his first preface that it "was professedly written in imitation of the *style,* as well as of the spirit of the elder poets." Coleridge did much more than imitate the old ballads. He made use of the typical and most effective features of balladry, such as the rapid movement, free interchange of metrical feet, repetition, alliteration, end rhyme and interlinear rhyme; but with the supreme artist's creative skill he worked these hackneyed elements into a new metrical structure that was quite his own and unique in poetry. He not only gave life to the old ballad, but gave to it a new life different from any that it had known before, a life endowed with music, magic expression and spiritual power. The typical ballad stanza consists of four lines, the first and third having four feet in each and no rhyme, the second and fourth having three feet with rhyme. The measure is iambic, varied with anapestic substitutions. Such is the first stanza of the *Ancient Mariner,* which will scan thus:

> It is an ancient mariner,
>   And he stoppeth one of three.
> By thy long grey beard and glittering eye,
>   Now wherefore stoppst thou me?

Coleridge used this stanza as a basis, modifying it in a variety of ways. He not only interchanged iambic and anapestic feet, but often substituted a trochee, as in 11. 29, 84, 119, 174. His use of interlinear rhyme is seen in such lines as 27, 31, 49, 53. This freedom was allowed in the older poetry, but in the eighteenth century it was an offense against the laws of poetry as understood in the school of Pope. Coleridge rebelled against the starched precision of the rhymed couplet and the tame uniformity of even the best verse of the century, like that of Gray's *Elegy*. This use of irregular meter he regarded as a "new principle," which is illustrated more fully in *Christabel;* and what he says in the preface to that poem in explanation of his departure applies equally to the *Ancient Mariner*.

CRITICISM OF THE ANCIENT MARINER

There can be no doubt that the *Ancient Mariner* at first shocked the general public, and pleased not even the poet's best friends. Its strangeness was utterly incomprehensible. Southey called it "a Dutch attempt at German sublimity," adding, "many of the stanzas are laboriously beautiful; but in connection they are absurd or unintelligible." A writer in the *Monthly Review* for June, 1799, reviewed the volume and said of the *Ancient Mariner:* "Though it seems a rhapsody of unintelligible wildness and incoherence (of which we do not perceive the drift, unless the joke lies in depriving the wedding-guest of his share of the feast), there are in it poetical touches of an exquisite kind." Even Wordsworth believed the failure of the volume to be due to the unpopularity of this initial ballad, and in the second edition added a curiously apologetic and patronizing note, giving his reasons for republishing it. "The poem of my friend," he says, "has indeed great defects: first, that the principal person has no distinct character, either in his profession of Mariner, or as a human being who having been long under the control of supernatural impressions might be supposed himself to partake of something supernatural; secondly, that he does not act, but is continually acted upon; thirdly, that the events having no necessary connection do not produce each other; and lastly, that the imagery is somewhat too laboriously accumulated. Yet the poem contains many delicate touches of passion, and indeed the passion is everywhere true to nature; a great number of the stanzas present beautiful images, and are expressed with unusual felicity of language; and the versification, though the meter is itself unfit for long poems, is harmonious and artfully varied." Therefore, it appeared to him that these several merits "gave to the poem a value which is not often possessed by better poems."

A century has passed and other Daniels have come to judgment. Says Campbell, "The *Ancient Mariner* is the one perfect, complete, and rounded poem of any length which Coleridge achieved." "As to its poetry," says Stopford Brooke, "it is like that of *Christabel,* not to be analyzed or explained. The spirit herself of Poetry is everywhere, in these two poems, felt, but never obtruding, touching spiritual life and earthly loveliness each with equal light, and so charming sense and soul with music that what is spiritual seems sensible, and what is of the senses seems spiritual."

The poet Swinburne regards this poem as "beyond question one of the supreme triumphs of poetry. . . . For the execution, I presume no human eye is too dull to see how perfect it is, and how high in kind of perfection. Here is not the speckless and elaborate finish which shows everywhere the fresh rasp of file or chisel on its smooth and spruce excellence; this is faultless after the fashion of a flower or a tree. Thus it has grown; not thus has it been carved."

And finally, we must listen to the high judgment of Lowell: "He has written some of the most poetical poetry in the language, and one poem, the *Ancient Mariner,* not only unparalleled, but unapproachable in its kind, and that kind of the rarest. It is marvelous in its mastery over that delightfully fortuitous inconsequence that is the adamantine logic of dream-land. Coleridge has taken the old ballad measure and given to it by an indefinable charm wholly his own all the sweetness, all the melody and compass of a symphony. And how picturesque it is in the proper sense of the word. I know nothing like it. There is not a description in it. It is all picture. Descriptive poets generally confuse us with multiplicity of detail; we cannot see their forest for the trees; but Coleridge never errs in this way. With instinctive tact he touches the right chord of association, and is satisfied, as we also are. I should find it hard to explain the singular charm of his diction, there is so much nicety of art and purpose in it, whether for music or meaning. Nor does it need any explanation, for we all feel it. The words seem common words enough, but in the order of them, in the choice, variety, and position of the vowel-sounds, they become magical. The most decrepit vocable in the language throws away its crutches to dance and sing at his piping."

CHRISTABEL

In 1816 a small pamphlet was published by John Murray, containing *Christabel, Kubla Khan,* and *The Pains of Sleep.* Byron, who already knew the poem in manuscript, advised the great publisher to print *Christabel,* saying, "I won't have any one sneer at *Christabel;* it is a fine wild poem." The pamphlet contained the following "Preface":

"The first part of the following poem was written in the year one thousand seven hundred and ninety-seven, at Stowey, in the county of Somerset. The second part, after my return from Germany, in the year one thousand eight hundred, at Keswick, Cumberland. Since the latter date, my poetic powers have been, till very lately, in a state of suspended animation. But, as in my very first conception of the tale, I had the whole present to my mind, with the wholeness, no less than with the liveliness, of a vision, I trust that I shall be able to embody in verse the three parts yet to come, in the course of the present year.

"It is probable that if the poem had been finished at either of the former periods, or if even the first and second part had been published in the year 1800, the impression of its originality would have been much greater than I dare at present expect. But for this, I have only my own indolence to blame. The dates are mentioned for the exclusive purpose of precluding charges of plagiarism or servile imitation from myself. For there is amongst us a set of critics who seem to hold that every possible thought and image is traditional; who have no notion that there are such things as fountains in the world, small as well as great; and who would therefore charitably derive every rill they behold flowing, from a perforation made in some other man's tank. I am confident, however, that as far as the present poem is concerned, the celebrated poets whose writings I might be suspected of having imitated, either in particular passages, or in the tone and the spirit of the whole, would be among the first to vindicate me from the charge, and who, on any striking coincidence, would permit me to address them in this doggerel version of two monkish Latin hexameters:

> 'Tis mine, and it is likewise yours;
> But an if this will not do,
> Let it be mine, good friend, for I
> Am the poorer of the two.

"I have only to add that the meter of the *Christabel* is not, properly speaking, irregular, though it may seem so from its being founded on a new principle,—namely, that of counting in each line the accents, not the syllables. Though the latter may vary from seven to twelve, yet in each line the accents will be found to be only four. Nevertheless, this occasional variation in number of syllables is not introduced wantonly, or for the mere ends of convenience, but in correspondence with some transition, in the nature of the imagery or passion."

The hope expressed at the end of the first paragraph was never fulfilled. These words were modified in subsequent editions, and finally in the edition of 1834 were omitted altogether. For many years he was constantly promising his friends and himself that he would complete the poem, yet it is doubtful whether at any time he could have done so successfully. The magic wand was broken. The clear and alluring light of romantic vision with which his creative soul was illuminated in that wonderful year at Stowey was never so pure and clear again. Even as soon as 1799 he began to be tormented with doubts. "I am afraid," he writes, "that I have scarce poetic enthusiasm enough to finish *Christabel.*" Yet the idea of finishing it haunted him all his life. In 1833 he said *(Table Talk,* July 6): "The reason of my not finishing *Christabel* is not that I don't know how to do it—for I have, as I always had, the whole plan entire from beginning to end in my mind; but I fear I could not carry on with equal success the execution of the idea, an extremely subtle and difficult one." And so the poem was left forever, as Scott called it, "a beautiful and tantalizing fragment."

Gillman, in his *Life of Coleridge,* gives the plan of a conclusion, as Coleridge "explained the story to his friends."

"The following relation was to have occupied a third and fourth canto, and to have closed the tale. Over the mountains the Bard, as directed by Sir Leoline, hastes with his disciple; but in consequence of one of those inundations, supposed to be common to this country, the spot only where the castle once stood is discovered, the edifice itself being washed away. He determines to return. Geraldine, being acquainted with all that is passing, like the weird sisters in *Macbeth,* vanishes. Reappearing, however, she awaits the return of the bard, exciting in the meantime, by her wily arts, all the anger she could rouse in the baron's breast, as well as that jealousy of which he is described to have been susceptible. The old Bard and the youth at length arrive, and therefore she can no longer personate the character of Geraldine, the daughter of Lord Roland de Vaux, but changes her appearance to that of the accepted though absent lover of Christabel. Next ensues a courtship most distressing to Christabel, who feels, she knows not why, great disgust for her once favored knight. This coldness is very painful to the Baron, who has no more conception than herself of the supernatural transformation. She at last yields to her father's entreaties, and consents to approach the altar with this hated suitor. The real lover, returning, enters at this moment, and produces the ring which she had once given him in sign of her betrothment. Thus defeated, the supernatural being, Geraldine, disappears. As predicted, the castle bell tolls, the mother's voice is heard, and to the exceeding great joy of the parties, the rightful marriage takes place, after which follows a reconciliation and explanation between the father and daughter."

This conclusion, says Rossetti, "I believe is correct enough, only not picturesquely worded. It does not seem a bad conclusion by any means, though it would require fine treatment to make it seem a really good one."

As to the meaning of the poem, it is very unlikely that Coleridge intended to embody in it any specific moral or psychological idea. Indeed, he himself called it just "a common Fairy tale." Nevertheless, it has a moral significance, as has all fine imaginative art, which is revealed variously through a refined symbolism to the inquiring spirits that are brought to its contemplation; but it would be as unsafe to insist upon any particular "interpretation" as to pronounce dogmatically upon the moral purpose of the *Laocoon* or the *Dying Gladiator.* Gillman inferred from Coleridge's conversation that the story is "partly founded on the notion that the virtuous of this world save the wicked." Campbell suggests that this explanation must have been "mere quizzing on the part of Coleridge, indulged in to relieve the pressure of prosaic curiosity." Each intelligent reader will extract from the poem a moral according to his own moral aptitude.

CRITICISM OF CHRISTABEL

The appeal of *Christabel* to the critics, in 1816, was not any more favorable than that of the *Ancient Mariner* in 1798. The *Edinburgh Review* said that it exhibited "from beginning to end not a ray of genius," and declared it to be "one of the most notable pieces of impertinence of which the press has lately been guilty; and one of the boldest experiments that has yet been made upon the patience and understanding of the public." Although the reception of the poem was disappointing, the pamphlet sold rapidly, and soon went into a second edition.

It is generally agreed that the second part of *Christabel* is inferior to the first. Coleridge himself seemed to feel this. "Certainly," he says, "the first canto is more perfect, has more of the true wild, weird spirit than the last." As we pass from the first to the second part, says Prof. Beers," the magic glamour has faded into the light of common day. . . . The fact that *Christabel* was left unfinished is not needed, as evidence, to prove that Coleridge could never have finished it in the spirit in which it was begun."

"The first part," says Prof. Herford, "is a masterpiece in the art of suggesting enchantment by purely natural means. The castle, the wood, the mastiff, the tree with its jagged shadows, are drawn with a quivering intensity of touch which conveys the very atmosphere of foreboding and suspense. The real marvel, too, when we come to it— the serpent-nature of Geraldine—is of a more searching and subtle weirdness than that of *The Mariner;* for no prodigies of the external world touch the imagination so nearly as distortions of human personality."

"The magical beauty of *Christabel,*" *s*ays J. C. Shairp, "has been so long canonized in the world's estimate that to praise it now would be unseemly. It brought into English poetry an atmosphere of wonder and mystery, of weird beauty and pity combined, which was quite new at the time it appeared, and has never since been approached. The movement of its subtle cadences has a union of grace with power which only the finest lines of Shakspere can parallel. As we read *Christabel* and a few other of Coleridge's pieces we recall his own words:

> 'In a half sleep we dream,
> And dreaming hear thee still, O singing lark!
> That singest like an angel in the clouds.'"

Lowell suggests a discriminating comparison, which is worth careful consideration. "I confess," he says, "that I prefer the *Ancient Mariner* to *Christabel,* fine as that poem is in parts and tantalizing as it is in the suggestion of deeper meanings than were ever there. The *Ancient Mariner* seems to have come of itself. In *Christabel* I fancy him saying, 'Go to, let us write an imaginative poem.' It could never be finished on those terms."

KUBLA KHAN

This poem was first printed in 1816, in the pamphlet with *Christabel,* with the title *Kubla Khan; or, A Vision in a Dream,* and with the following prefatory explanation by Coleridge:

"The following fragment is here published at the request of a poet of great and deserved celebrity, and as far as the author's own opinions are concerned, rather as a psychological curiosity than on the ground of any supposed *poetic* merits.

"In the summer of the year 1797, the author, then in ill health, had retired to a lonely farm-house between Porlock and Linton, on the Exmoor confines of Somerset and Devonshire. In consequence of a slight indisposition, an anodyne had been prescribed, from the effects of which he fell asleep in his chair at the moment that he was reading the following sentence, or words of the same substance, in *Purchas's Pilgrimage:* 'Here the Khan Kubla commanded a palace to be built, and a stately garden thereunto. And thus ten miles of fertile ground was inclosed with a wall.' The author continued for about three hours in a profound sleep, at least of the external senses, during which time he has the most vivid confidence that he could not have composed less than from two to three hundred lines; if that indeed can be called composition in which all the images rose up before him as *things,* with a parallel production of the correspondent expressions, without any sensation or consciousness of effort. On awaking he appeared to himself to have a distinct recollection of the whole, and taking his pen, ink, and paper, instantly and eagerly wrote down the lines that are here preserved. At this moment he was unfortunately called out by a person on business from Porlock, and detained by him above an hour, and on his return to his room, found, to his no small surprise and mortification, that though he still retained some vague and dim recollection of the general purport of the vision, yet, with the exception of some eight or ten scattered lines and images, all the rest had passed away like the images on the surface of a stream into which a stone has been cast, but, alas! without the after restoration of the latter!

> Then all the charm
> Is broken—all that phantom-world so fair
> Vanishes, and a thousand circlets spread,
> And each mis-shape the other. Stay awhile,
> Poor youth! who scarcely dar'st lift up thine eyes—
> The stream will soon renew its smoothness, soon
> The visions will return! And lo! he stays,
> And soon the fragments dim of lovely forms
> Come trembling back, unite, and now once more
> The pool becomes a mirror.

"Yet from the still surviving recollections in his mind, the author has frequently purposed to finish for himself what had been originally, as it were, given to him. Αὔριον ἄδιον ἄσω; but the to-morrow is yet to come."

The celebrated poet referred to in the first paragraph was Byron. The experience with the anodyne was probably one of the first, if not the first, of Coleridge's experiences with the strange effects of opium. All of his great poems are, in a sense, miraculous productions. The dream element is in them all; but how much the marvelous drug may have had to do with the dreams we shall never know. In April, 1816, Lamb wrote to Wordsworth:

"Coleridge is printing *Christabel* by Lord Byron's recommendation to Murray, with what he calls a vision, *Kubla Khan,* which said vision he repeats so enchantingly that it irradiates and brings heaven and elysian bowers into my parlor when he sings or says it; but there is an observation, 'Never tell thy dreams,' and I am almost afraid that *Kubla Khan* is an owl that will not bear daylight. I fear lest it should be discovered by the lantern of typography and clear reducting to letters no better than nonsense or no sense."

The *Edinburgh Review* thought *Kubla Khan* not quite so bad as *Christabel,* and not "mere raving" like *The Pains of Sleep,* but bad enough to be condemned. Compare this judgment with that of Swinburne, who pronounces *Kubla Khan* to be "for absolute melody and splendor, the first poem in the language." Here we have the beginning and the end of criticism upon this marvelous fragment of poetic melody. Let the imagination yield freely to the fascination of the dream pictures, with no attempt to compel the lines to give forth a coherent meaning, and the judgment of Swinburne, within the limitations he names, will not seem extravagant.

DEJECTION: AN ODE

Few personal poems possess the profound interest of this ode, which is not an ode *to* dejection, contemplated poetically, but an expression of dejection as actually experienced. It is a confession from out of the depths of a heavily burdened soul, and the pain and pathos of its yearning and despairing lines are increased by the consciousness that the burden was largely of that soul's own creating. Ill health, domestic tribulation, and the opium indulgence combined to produce the mood in which the poem was written. Nor was it the expression of a passing mood, as Traill suggests, like that of Shelley's poem of the same title, but rather "the record of a life change, a veritable threnody over a spiritual death. For there can be no doubt—his whole subsequent history goes to show it—that Coleridge's 'shaping spirit of Imagination' was in fact dead when these lines were written. To a man of stronger moral fiber a renascence of the poetical instinct in other forms might have been possible; but the poet of *Christabel* and the *Ancient Mariner* was dead. The metaphysician had taken his place, and was striving, in abstruse research, to live in forgetfulness of the loss."

The poem was first printed in the *Morning Post,* Oct. 4, 1802, which was Wordsworth's wedding-day. As originally written, it was addressed to Wordsworth, the name "William" appearing throughout the poem in the lines of personal address. But in the first printed form this name was changed to "Edmund," and this again was changed in the edition of 1817 to the present "Lady," referring presumably (if any personal reference is intended) to Mrs. Wordsworth, or Dorothy Wordsworth. Many other changes were made in the poem in 1817, some of which are described in the notes. The complete poem in its first printed form is given in the Appendix to Campbell's edition; as first written, it is given by Coleridge in a letter to W. Sotheby, July 19, 1802 (See *Letters,* Vol. I, pp. 378-384). Coleridge's reason for blotting out all direct allusions to Wordsworth is an unsolved problem. In 1802 Wordsworth was his most intimate friend,—"friend of my devoutest choice"—and the personal passages in the poem are a noble tribute of admiration to this friend. Campbell thinks that the explanation is found in a temporary estrangement between the two friends that occurred between 1802 and 1817, the reconciliation not having cleared away entirely "the marks of that which once had been." In the same manner he removed the personal color from his poem, *To William Wordsworth,* composed on hearing Wordsworth recite the *Prelude,* the title becoming *To a Gentleman.*

It is quite possible, however, that for the artistic and permanent purposes of poetry Coleridge concluded that the personal coloring should be more obscure; upon this basis the "Lady" of the ode would be merely an impersonal idealization of lofty character. The matter is discussed briefly in the notes, and an interesting discussion of the whole question by Canon Ainger may be found in *Macmillan's Magazine,* June, 1887. The other poems recording the friendship of these two great poets should be read in connection with this ode, Coleridge's *To a Gentleman,* just mentioned, and Wordsworth's *Stanzas Written in my Pocket-copy of Thomson's "*C*astle of Indolence,"* and the last book of the *Prelude,* especially the concluding passage beginning:

"Whether to me shall be allotted life," etc.

JULIAN B. ABERNETHY.

1907.

The Rime of the Ancient Mariner

[1797-98, REVISED LATER; MARGINAL GLOSSES ADDED 1815-16]

IN SEVEN PARTS

Facile credo, plures esse Naturas invisibiles quam visibiles in rerum universitate. Sed horum omnium familiam quis nobis enarrabit? et gradus et cognationes et discrimina et singulorum munera? Quid agunt? quae loca habitant? Harum rerum notitiam semper ambivit ingenium humanum, nunquam attigit. Juvat, interea, non diffiteor, quandoque in animo, tanquam in tabulâ, majoris et melioris mundi imaginem contemplari: ne mens assuefacta hodiernae vitae minutiis se contrahat nimis, et tota subsidat in pusillas cogitationes. Sed veritati interea invigilandum est, modusque servandus, ut certa ab incertis, diem a nocte, distinguamus.—T. Burnet, Archaeol. Phil., p. 68[1]

Argument

How a Ship having passed the Line was driven by storms to the cold Country towards the South Pole; and how from thence she made her course to the tropical Latitude of the Great Pacific Ocean; and of the strange things that befell; and in what manner the Ancyent Marinere came back to his own Country.

Part I

It is an ancient Mariner,[2]
And he stoppeth one of three.
'By thy long beard and glittering eye,
Now wherefore stopp'st thou me?

---

[1] Translation: "I can easily believe, that there are more invisible than visible Beings in the universe. But who shall describe for us their families? and their ranks and relationships and distinguishing features and functions? What they do? where they live? The human mind has always circled around a knowledge of these things, never attaining it. I do not doubt, however, that it is sometimes beneficial to contemplate, in thought, as in a Picture, the image of a greater and better world; lest the intellect, habituated to the trivia of daily life, may contract itself too much, and wholly sink into trifles. But at the same time we must be vigilant for truth, and maintain proportion, that we may distinguish certain from uncertain, day from night."

[2] An ancient Mariner meeteth three Gallants bidden to a wedding-feast, and detaineth one.

The Bridegroom's doors are opened wide,
And I am next of kin;
The guests are met, the feast is set:
May'st hear the merry din.'

He holds him with his skinny hand,
'There was a ship,' quoth he.
'Hold off! unhand me, grey-beard loon!'
Eftsoons his hand dropt he.

He holds him with his glittering eye—[3]
The Wedding-Guest stood still,
And listens like a three years' child:
The Mariner hath his will.

The Wedding-Guest sat on a stone:
He cannot choose but hear;
And thus spake on that ancient man,
The bright-eyed Mariner.

'The ship was cheered, the harbour cleared,
Merrily did we drop
Below the kirk, below the hill,
Below the lighthouse top.

The Sun came up upon the left,[4]
Out of the sea came he!
And he shone bright, and on the right
Went down into the sea.

Higher and higher every day,
Till over the mast at noon—'
The Wedding-Guest here beat his breast,
For he heard the loud bassoon.

---

[3] The Wedding-Guest is spell-bound by the eye of the old seafaring man, and constrained to hear his tale.

[4] The Mariner tells how the ship sailed southward with a good wind and fair weather, till it reached the Line.

The bride hath paced into the hall,[5]
Red as a rose is she;
Nodding their heads before her goes
The merry minstrelsy.

The Wedding-Guest he beat his breast,
Yet he cannot choose but hear;
And thus spake on that ancient man,
The bright-eyed Mariner.

And now the storm-blast came, and he[6]
Was tyrannous and strong:
He struck with his o'ertaking wings,
And chased us south along.

With sloping masts and dipping prow,
As who pursued with yell and blow
Still treads the shadow of his foe,
And forward bends his head,
The ship drove fast, loud roared the blast,
The southward aye we fled.

And now there came both mist and snow,
And it grew wondrous cold:
And ice, mast-high, came floating by,
As green as emerald.

And through the drifts the snowy clifts[7]
Did send a dismal sheen:
Nor shapes of men nor beasts we ken—
The ice was all between.

The ice was here, the ice was there,
The ice was all around:
It cracked and growled, and roared and howled,
Like noises in a swound!

---

[5] The Wedding-Guest heareth the bridal music; but the Mariner continueth his tale.
[6] The ship driven by a storm toward the south pole.
[7] The land of ice, and of fearful sounds where no living thing was to be seen.

At length did cross an Albatross,[8]
Thorough the fog it came;
As if it had been a Christian soul,
We hailed it in God's name.

It ate the food it ne'er had eat,
And round and round it flew.
The ice did split with a thunder-fit;
The helmsman steered us through!

And a good south wind sprung up behind;[9]
The Albatross did follow,
And every day, for food or play,
Came to the mariner's hollo!

In mist or cloud, on mast or shroud,
It perched for vespers nine;
Whiles all the night, through fog-smoke white,
Glimmered the white Moon-shine.'

The ancient Mariner inhospitably killeth the pious bird of good omen.
'God save thee, ancient Mariner!
From the fiends, that plague thee thus!—
Why look'st thou so?'—With my cross-bow
I shot the Albatross.

Part II

The Sun now rose upon the right:
Out of the sea came he,
Still hid in mist, and on the left
Went down into the sea.

And the good south wind still blew behind,
But no sweet bird did follow,
Nor any day for food or play
Came to the mariners' hollo!

---

[8] Till a great sea-bird, called the Albatross, came through the snow-fog, and was received with great joy and hospitality.

[9] And lo! the Albatross proveth a bird of good omen, and followeth the ship as it returned northward through fog and floating ice.

And I had done an hellish thing,[10]
And it would work 'em woe:
For all averred, I had killed the bird
That made the breeze to blow.
Ah wretch! said they, the bird to slay,
That made the breeze to blow!

Nor dim nor red, like God's own head,[11]
The glorious Sun uprist:
Then all averred, I had killed the bird
That brought the fog and mist.
'Twas right, said they, such birds to slay,
That bring the fog and mist.

The fair breeze blew, the white foam flew,[12]
The furrow followed free;
We were the first that ever burst
Into that silent sea.

Down dropt the breeze, the sails dropt down,[13]
'Twas sad as sad could be;
And we did speak only to break
The silence of the sea!

All in a hot and copper sky,
The bloody Sun, at noon,
Right up above the mast did stand,
No bigger than the Moon.

Day after day, day after day,
We stuck, nor breath nor motion;
As idle as a painted ship
Upon a painted ocean.

---

[10] His shipmates cry out against the ancient Mariner, for killing the bird of good luck.
[11] But when the fog cleared off, they justify the same, and thus make themselves accomplices in the crime.
[12] The fair breeze continues; the ship enters the Pacific Ocean, and sails northward, even till it reaches the Line.
[13] The ship hath been suddenly becalmed.

Water, water, every where,[14]
And all the boards did shrink;
Water, water, every where,
Nor any drop to drink.

The very deep did rot: O Christ!
That ever this should be!
Yea, slimy things did crawl with legs
Upon the slimy sea.

About, about, in reel and rout
The death-fires danced at night;
The water, like a witch's oils,
Burnt green, and blue and white.

And some in dreams assured were[15]
Of the Spirit that plagued us so;
Nine fathom deep he had followed us
From the land of mist and snow.

And every tongue, through utter drought,
Was withered at the root;
We could not speak, no more than if
We had been choked with soot.

Ah! well a-day! what evil looks[16]
Had I from old and young!
Instead of the cross, the Albatross
About my neck was hung.

---

[14] And the Albatross begins to be avenged.

[15] A Spirit had followed them; one of the invisible inhabitants of this planet, neither departed souls nor angels; concerning whom the learned Jew, Josephus, and the Platonic Constantinopolitan, Michael Psellus, may be consulted. They are very numerous, and there is no climate or element without one or more.

[16] The shipmates, in their sore distress, would fain throw the whole guilt on the ancient Mariner: in sign whereof they hang the dead sea-bird round his neck.

Part III

There passed a weary time. Each throat
Was parched, and glazed each eye.
A weary time! a weary time!
How glazed each weary eye,
When looking westward, I beheld[17]
A something in the sky.

At first it seemed a little speck,
And then it seemed a mist;
It moved and moved, and took at last
A certain shape, I wist.

A speck, a mist, a shape, I wist!
And still it neared and neared:
As if it dodged a water-sprite,
It plunged and tacked and veered.

With throats unslaked, with black lips baked,[18]
We could nor laugh nor wail;
Through utter drought all dumb we stood!
I bit my arm, I sucked the blood,
And cried, A sail! a sail!

With throats unslaked, with black lips baked,[19]
Agape they heard me call:
Gramercy! they for joy did grin,
And all at once their breath drew in,
As they were drinking all.

See! see! (I cried) she tacks no more![20]
Hither to work us weal;
Without a breeze, without a tide,
She steadies with upright keel!

---

[17] The ancient Mariner beholdeth a sign in the element afar off.

[18] At its nearer approach, it seemeth him to be a ship; and at a dear ransom he freeth his speech from the bonds of thirst.

[19] A flash of joy;

[20] And horror follows. For can it be a ship that comes onward without wind or tide?

The western wave was all a-flame.
The day was well nigh done!
Almost upon the western wave
Rested the broad bright Sun;
When that strange shape drove suddenly[21]
Betwixt us and the Sun.

And straight the Sun was flecked with bars,[22]
(Heaven's Mother send us grace!)
As if through a dungeon-grate he peered
With broad and burning face.

Alas! (thought I, and my heart beat loud)
How fast she nears and nears!
Are those her sails that glance in the Sun,
Like restless gossameres?

Are those her ribs through which the Sun[23]
Did peer, as through a grate?
And is that Woman all her crew?
Is that a death? and are there two?
Is death that woman's mate?

[FIRST VERSION OF THIS STANZA THROUGH THE END OF PART III.]

Her lips were red, her looks were free,[24]
Her locks were yellow as gold:
Her skin was as white as leprosy,
The Night-mare Life-in-Death was she,
Who thicks man's blood with cold.

The naked hulk alongside came,[25]
And the twain were casting dice;
'The game is done! I've won! I've won!'
Quoth she, and whistles thrice.

---

[21] It seemeth him but the skeleton of a ship.
[22] And its ribs are seen as bars on the face of the setting Sun.
[23] The Spectre-Woman and her Death-mate, and no other on board the skeleton ship.
[24] Like vessel, like crew!
[25] Death and Life-in-Death have diced for the ship's crew, and she (the latter) winneth the ancient Mariner.

The Sun's rim dips; the stars rush out:[26]
At one stride comes the dark;
With far-heard whisper, o'er the sea,
Off shot the spectre-bark.

We listened and looked sideways up!
Fear at my heart, as at a cup,
My life-blood seemed to sip!
The stars were dim, and thick the night,[27]
The steerman's face by his lamp gleamed white;
From the sails the dew did drip—
Till clomb above the eastern bar
The hornéd Moon, with one bright star
Within the nether tip.

One after one, by the star-dogged Moon,[28]
Too quick for groan or sigh,
Each turned his face with a ghastly pang,
And cursed me with his eye.

Four times fifty living men,[29]
(And I heard nor sigh nor groan)
With heavy thump, a lifeless lump,
They dropped down one by one.

The souls did from their bodies fly,[30]
They fled to bliss or woe!
And every soul, it passed me by,
Like the whizz of my cross-bow!

Part IV

'I fear thee, ancient Mariner!'[31]
I fear thy skinny hand!
And thou art long, and lank, and brown,
As is the ribbed sea-sand.

---

[26] No twilight within the courts of the Sun.
[27] At the rising of the Moon,
[28] One after another,
[29] His shipmates drop down dead.
[30] But Life-in-Death begins her work on the ancient Mariner.
[31] The Wedding-Guest feareth that a Spirit is talking to him;

I fear thee and thy glittering eye,
And thy skinny hand, so brown.'—
Fear not, fear not, thou Wedding-Guest![32]
This body dropt not down.

Alone, alone, all, all alone,
Alone on a wide wide sea!
And never a saint took pity on
My soul in agony.

The many men, so beautiful![33]
And they all dead did lie:
And a thousand thousand slimy things
Lived on; and so did I.

I looked upon the rotting sea,
And drew my eyes away;
I looked upon the rotting deck,
And there the dead men lay.[34]

I looked to heaven, and tried to pray;
But or ever a prayer had gusht,
A wicked whisper came, and made
My heart as dry as dust.

I closed my lids, and kept them close,
And the balls like pulses beat;
For the sky and the sea, and the sea and the sky
Lay like a load on my weary eye,
And the dead were at my feet.

The cold sweat melted from their limbs,
Nor rot nor reek did they:
The look with which they looked on me[35]
Had never passed away.

---

[32] But the ancient Mariner assureth him of his bodily life, and proceedeth to relate his horrible penance.
[33] He despiseth the creatures of the calm,
[34] And envieth that they should live, and so many lie dead.
[35] But the curse liveth for him in the eye of the dead men.

An orphan's curse would drag to hell
A spirit from on high;
But oh! more horrible than that
Is the curse in a dead man's eye!
Seven days, seven nights, I saw that curse,
And yet I could not die.

The moving Moon went up the sky,[36]
And no where did abide:
Softly she was going up,
And a star or two beside—

Her beams bemocked the sultry main,
Like April hoar-frost spread;
But where the ship's huge shadow lay,
The charméd water burnt alway
A still and awful red.

Beyond the shadow of the ship,[37]
I watched the water-snakes:
They moved in tracks of shining white,
And when they reared, the elfish light
Fell off in hoary flakes.

Within the shadow of the ship
I watched their rich attire:
Blue, glossy green, and velvet black,
They coiled and swam; and every track
Was a flash of golden fire.

O happy living things! no tongue[38]
Their beauty might declare:
A spring of love gushed from my heart,
And I blessed them unaware:[39]
Sure my kind saint took pity on me,
And I blessed them unaware.

---

[36] In his loneliness and fixedness he yearneth towards the journeying Moon, and the stars that still sojourn, yet still move onward; and every where the blue sky belongs to them, and is their appointed rest, and their native country and their own natural homes, which they enter unannounced, as lords that are certainly expected and yet there is a silent joy at their arrival.

[37] By the light of the Moon he beholdeth God's creatures of the great calm.

[38] Their beauty and their happiness.

[39] He blesseth them in his heart.

The self-same moment I could pray;
And from my neck so free
The Albatross fell off, and sunk[40]
Like lead into the sea.

Part V

Oh sleep! it is a gentle thing,
Beloved from pole to pole!
To Mary Queen the praise be given!
She sent the gentle sleep from Heaven,
That slid into my soul.

The silly buckets on the deck,[41]
That had so long remained,
I dreamt that they were filled with dew;
And when I awoke, it rained.

My lips were wet, my throat was cold,
My garments all were dank;
Sure I had drunken in my dreams,
And still my body drank.

I moved, and could not feel my limbs:
I was so light—almost
I thought that I had died in sleep,
And was a blessèd ghost.

And soon I heard a roaring wind:[42]
It did not come anear;
But with its sound it shook the sails,
That were so thin and sere.

The upper air burst into life!
And a hundred fire-flags sheen,
To and fro they were hurried about!
And to and fro, and in and out,
The wan stars danced between.

---

[40] The spell begins to break.
[41] By grace of the holy Mother, the ancient Mariner is refreshed with rain.
[42] He heareth sounds and seeth strange sights and commotions in the sky and the element.

And the coming wind did roar more loud,
And the sails did sigh like sedge;
And the rain poured down from one black cloud;
The Moon was at its edge.

The thick black cloud was cleft, and still
The Moon was at its side:
Like waters shot from some high crag,
The lightning fell with never a jag,
A river steep and wide.

The loud wind never reached the ship,
Yet now the ship moved on!
Beneath the lightning and the moon[43]
The dead men gave a groan.

They groaned, they stirred, they all uprose,
Nor spake, nor moved their eyes;
It had been strange, even in a dream,
To have seen those dead men rise.

The helmsman steered, the ship moved on;
Yet never a breeze up-blew;
The mariners all 'gan work the ropes,
Where they were wont to do;
They raised their limbs like lifeless tools—
We were a ghastly crew.

The body of my brother's son
Stood by me, knee to knee:
The body and I pulled at one rope,
But he said nought to me.

'I fear thee, ancient Mariner!'
Be calm, thou Wedding-Guest!
'Twas not those souls that fled in pain,[44]
Which to their corses came again,
But a troop of spirits blest:

---

[43] The bodies of the ship's crew are inspired, and the ship moves on;

[44] But not by the souls of the men, nor by dæmons of earth or middle air, but by a blessed troop of angelic spirits, sent down by the invocation of the guardian saint.

Samuel Taylor Coleridge 45

For when it dawned—they dropped their arms,
And clustered round the mast;
Sweet sounds rose slowly through their mouths,
And from their bodies passed.

Around, around, flew each sweet sound,
Then darted to the Sun;
Slowly the sounds came back again,
Now mixed, now one by one.

Sometimes a-dropping from the sky
I heard the sky-lark sing;
Sometimes all little birds that are,
How they seemed to fill the sea and air
With their sweet jargoning!

And now 'twas like all instruments,
Now like a lonely flute;
And now it is an angel's song,
That makes the heavens be mute.

It ceased; yet still the sails made on
A pleasant noise till noon,
A noise like of a hidden brook
In the leafy month of June,
That to the sleeping woods all night
Singeth a quiet tune.

[ADDITIONAL STANZAS, DROPPED AFTER THE FIRST EDITION.]

Till noon we quietly sailed on,
Yet never a breeze did breathe:
Slowly and smoothly went the ship,
Moved onward from beneath.

Under the keel nine fathom deep,[45]
From the land of mist and snow,
The spirit slid: and it was he
That made the ship to go.
The sails at noon left off their tune,
And the ship stood still also.

---

[45] The lonesome Spirit from the south-pole carries on the ship as far as the Line, in obedience to the angelic troop, but still requireth vengeance.

The Sun, right up above the mast,
Had fixed her to the ocean:
But in a minute she 'gan stir,
With a short uneasy motion—
Backwards and forwards half her length
With a short uneasy motion.

Then like a pawing horse let go,
She made a sudden bound:
It flung the blood into my head,
And I fell down in a swound.

How long in that same fit I lay,[46]
I have not to declare;
But ere my living life returned,
I heard and in my soul discerned
Two voices in the air.

'Is it he?' quoth one, 'Is this the man?
By him who died on cross,
With his cruel bow he laid full low
The harmless Albatross.

The spirit who bideth by himself
In the land of mist and snow,
He loved the bird that loved the man
Who shot him with his bow.'

The other was a softer voice,
As soft as honey-dew:
Quoth he, 'The man hath penance done,
And penance more will do.'

---

[46] The Polar Spirit's fellow-dæmons, the invisible inhabitants of the element, take part in his wrong; and two of them relate, one to the other, that penance long and heavy for the ancient Mariner hath been accorded to the Polar Spirit, who returneth southward.

Part VI

FIRST VOICE

'But tell me, tell me! speak again,
Thy soft response renewing—
What makes that ship drive on so fast?
What is the ocean doing?'

SECOND VOICE

'Still as a slave before his lord,
The ocean hath no blast;
His great bright eye most silently
Up to the Moon is cast—

If he may know which way to go;
For she guides him smooth or grim.
See, brother, see! how graciously
She looketh down on him.'

FIRST VOICE

'But why drives on that ship so fast,[47]
Without or wave or wind?'

SECOND VOICE

'The air is cut away before,
And closes from behind.

Fly, brother, fly! more high, more high!
Or we shall be belated:
For slow and slow that ship will go,
When the Mariner's trance is abated.'

I woke, and we were sailing on,[48]
As in a gentle weather:
'Twas night, calm night, the moon was high;
The dead men stood together.

---

[47] The Mariner hath been cast into a trance; for the angelic power causeth the vessel to drive northward faster than human life could endure.

[48] The supernatural motion is retarded; the Mariner awakes, and his penance begins anew.

All stood together on the deck,
For a charnel-dungeon fitter:
All fixed on me their stony eyes,
That in the Moon did glitter.

The pang, the curse, with which they died,
Had never passed away:
I could not draw my eyes from theirs,
Nor turn them up to pray.

And now this spell was snapt: once more[49]
I viewed the ocean green,
And looked far forth, yet little saw
Of what had else been seen—

Like one, that on a lonesome road
Doth walk in fear and dread,
And having once turned round walks on,
And turns no more his head;
Because he knows, a frightful fiend
Doth close behind him tread.

But soon there breathed a wind on me,
Nor sound nor motion made:
Its path was not upon the sea,
In ripple or in shade.

It raised my hair, it fanned my cheek
Like a meadow-gale of spring—
It mingled strangely with my fears,
Yet it felt like a welcoming.

Swiftly, swiftly flew the ship,
Yet she sailed softly too:
Sweetly, sweetly blew the breeze—
On me alone it blew.

Oh! dream of joy! is this indeed,[50]
The light-house top I see?
Is this the hill? is this the kirk?
Is this mine own countree?

---

[49] The curse is finally expiated.
[50] And the ancient Mariner beholdeth his native country.

We drifted o'er the harbour-bar,
And I with sobs did pray—
O let me be awake, my God!
Or let me sleep alway.

The harbour-bay was clear as glass,
So smoothly it was strewn!
And on the bay the moonlight lay,
And the shadow of the Moon.

[ADDITIONAL STANZAS, DROPPED AFTER THE FIRST EDITION.]

The rock shone bright, the kirk no less,
That stands above the rock:
The moonlight steeped in silentness
The steady weathercock.

And the bay was white with silent light,[51]
Till rising from the same,
Full many shapes, that shadows were,
In crimson colours came.

A little distance from the prow[52]
Those crimson shadows were:
I turned my eyes upon the deck—
Oh, Christ! what saw I there!

Each corse lay flat, lifeless and flat,
And, by the holy rood!
A man all light, a seraph-man,
On every corse there stood.

This seraph-band, each waved his hand:
It was a heavenly sight!
They stood as signals to the land,
Each one a lovely light;

This seraph-band, each waved his hand,
No voice did they impart—
No voice; but oh! the silence sank
Like music on my heart.

---

[51] The angelic spirits leave the dead bodies,
[52] And appear in their own forms of light.

But soon I heard the dash of oars,
I heard the Pilot's cheer;
My head was turned perforce away
And I saw a boat appear.

[ADDITIONAL STANZA, DROPPED AFTER THE FIRST EDITION.]

The Pilot and the Pilot's boy,
I heard them coming fast:
Dear Lord in Heaven! it was a joy
The dead men could not blast.

I saw a third—I heard his voice:
It is the Hermit good!
He singeth loud his godly hymns
That he makes in the wood.
He'll shrieve my soul, he'll wash away
The Albatross's blood.

Part VII

This Hermit good lives in that wood[53]
Which slopes down to the sea.
How loudly his sweet voice he rears!
He loves to talk with marineres
That come from a far countree.

He kneels at morn, and noon, and eve—
He hath a cushion plump:
It is the moss that wholly hides
The rotted old oak-stump.

The skiff-boat neared: I heard them talk,
'Why, this is strange, I trow!
Where are those lights so many and fair,
That signal made but now?'

---

[53] The Hermit of the Wood,

'Strange, by my faith!' the Hermit said—[54]
'And they answered not our cheer!
The planks looked warped! and see those sails,
How thin they are and sere!
I never saw aught like to them,
Unless perchance it were.

'Brown skeletons of leaves that lag
My forest-brook along;
When the ivy-tod is heavy with snow,
And the owlet whoops to the wolf below,
That eats the she-wolf's young.'

'Dear Lord! it hath a fiendish look—
(The Pilot made reply)
I am a-feared'—'Push on, push on!'
Said the Hermit cheerily.

The boat came closer to the ship,
But I nor spake nor stirred;
The boat came close beneath the ship,
And straight a sound was heard.

Under the water it rumbled on,
Still louder and more dread:
It reached the ship, it split the bay;
The ship went down like lead.[55]

Stunned by that loud and dreadful sound,[56]
Which sky and ocean smote,
Like one that hath been seven days drowned
My body lay afloat;
But swift as dreams, myself I found
Within the Pilot's boat.

Upon the whirl, where sank the ship,
The boat spun round and round;
And all was still, save that the hill
Was telling of the sound.

---

[54] Approacheth the ship with wonder.
[55] The ship suddenly sinketh.
[56] The ancient Mariner is saved in the Pilot's boat.

I moved my lips—the Pilot shrieked
And fell down in a fit;
The holy Hermit raised his eyes,
And prayed where he did sit.

I took the oars: the Pilot's boy,
Who now doth crazy go,
Laughed loud and long, and all the while
His eyes went to and fro.
'Ha! ha!' quoth he, 'full plain I see,
The Devil knows how to row.'

And now, all in my own countree,
I stood on the firm land!
The Hermit stepped forth from the boat,
And scarcely he could stand.

'O shrieve me, shrieve me, holy man!'[57]
The Hermit crossed his brow.
'Say quick,' quoth he, 'I bid thee say—
What manner of man art thou?'

Forthwith this frame of mine was wrenched
With a woful agony,
Which forced me to begin my tale;
And then it left me free.

Since then, at an uncertain hour,
That agony returns:
And till my ghastly tale is told,
This heart within me burns.

I pass, like night, from land to land;[58]
I have strange power of speech;
That moment that his face I see,
I know the man that must hear me:
To him my tale I teach.

---

[57] The ancient Mariner earnestly entreateth the Hermit to shrieve him; and the penance of life falls on him.

[58] And ever and anon through out his future life an agony constraineth him to travel from land to land;

What loud uproar bursts from that door!
The wedding-guests are there:
But in the garden-bower the bride
And bride-maids singing are:
And hark the little vesper bell,
Which biddeth me to prayer!

O Wedding-Guest! this soul hath been
Alone on a wide wide sea:
So lonely 'twas, that God himself
Scarce seeméd there to be.

O sweeter than the marriage-feast,
'Tis sweeter far to me,
To walk together to the kirk
With a goodly company!—

To walk together to the kirk,
And all together pray,
While each to his great Father bends,
Old men, and babes, and loving friends
And youths and maidens gay!

Farewell, farewell! but this I tell[59]
To thee, thou Wedding-Guest!
He prayeth well, who loveth well
Both man and bird and beast.

He prayeth best, who loveth best
All things both great and small;
For the dear God who loveth us,
He made and loveth all.

The Mariner, whose eye is bright,
Whose beard with age is hoar,
Is gone: and now the Wedding-Guest
Turned from the bridegroom's door.

---

[59] And to teach, by his own example, love and reverence to all things that God made and loveth.

He went like one that hath been stunned,
And is of sense forlorn:
A sadder and a wiser man,
He rose the morrow morn.

Kubla Khan

[1798]

OR, A VISION IN A DREAM. A FRAGMENT.

The following fragment is here published at the request of a poet of great and deserved celebrity [Lord Byron], and, as far as the Author's own opinions are concerned, rather as a psychological curiosity, than on the ground of any supposed poetic merits.

In the summer of the year 1797, the Author, then in ill health, had retired to a lonely farm-house between Porlock and Linton, on the Exmoor confines of Somerset and Devonshire. In consequence of a slight indisposition, an anodyne had been prescribed, from the effects of which he fell asleep in his chair at the moment that he was reading the following sentence, or words of the same substance, in Purchas's Pilgrimage: "Here the Khan Kubla commanded a palace to be built, and a stately garden thereunto. And thus ten miles of fertile ground were inclosed with a wall." The Author continued for about three hours in a profound sleep, at least of the external senses, during which time he has the most vivid confidence, that he could not have composed less than from two to three hundred lines; if that indeed can be called composition in which all the images rose up before him as things, with a parallel production of the correspondent expressions, without any sensation or consciousness of effort. On awakening he appeared to himself to have a distinct recollection of the whole, and taking his pen, ink, and paper, instantly and eagerly wrote down the lines that are here preserved. At this moment he was unfortunately called out by a person on business from Porlock, and detained by him above an hour, and on his return to his room, found, to his no small surprise and mortification, that though he still retained some vague and dim recollection of the general purport of the vision, yet, with the exception of some eight or ten scattered lines and images, all the rest had passed away like the images on the surface of a stream into which a stone has been cast, but, alas! without the after restoration of the latter!

> Then all the charm
> Is broken—all that phantom-world so fair
> Vanishes, and a thousand circlets spread,
> And each mis-shape the other. Stay awhile,
> Poor youth! who scarcely dar'st lift up thine eyes—
> The stream will soon renew its smoothness, soon
> The visions will return! And lo, he stays,
> And soon the fragments dim of lovely forms
> Come trembling back, unite, and now once more
> The pool becomes a mirror.

Yet from the still surviving recollections in his mind, the Author has frequently purposed to finish for himself what had been originally, as it were, given to him. Σαμερον αδιον ασω [Αΰριον άσω 1834]: but the to-morrow is yet to come.

As a contrast to this vision, I have annexed a fragment of a very different character, describing with equal fidelity the dream of pain and disease.

KUBLA KHAN

In Xanadu did Kubla Khan
A stately pleasure-dome decree:
Where Alph, the sacred river, ran
Through caverns measureless to man
   Down to a sunless sea.
So twice five miles of fertile ground
With walls and towers were girdled round:
And there were gardens bright with sinuous rills,
Where blossomed many an incense-bearing tree;
And here were forests ancient as the hills,
Enfolding sunny spots of greenery.

But oh! that deep romantic chasm which slanted
Down the green hill athwart a cedarn cover!
A savage place! as holy and enchanted
As e'er beneath a waning moon was haunted
By woman wailing for her demon-lover!
And from this chasm, with ceaseless turmoil seething,
As if this earth in fast thick pants were breathing,
A mighty fountain momently was forced:
Amid whose swift half-intermitted burst
Huge fragments vaulted like rebounding hail,
Or chaffy grain beneath the thresher's flail:

And 'mid these dancing rocks at once and ever
It flung up momently the sacred river.
Five miles meandering with a mazy motion
Through wood and dale the sacred river ran,
Then reached the caverns measureless to man,
And sank in tumult to a lifeless ocean:
And 'mid this tumult Kubla heard from far
Ancestral voices prophesying war!
   The shadow of the dome of pleasure
     Floated midway on the waves;
     Where was heard the mingled measure
     From the fountain and the caves.
It was a miracle of rare device,
A sunny pleasure-dome with caves of ice!

   A damsel with a dulcimer
   In a vision once I saw:
   It was an Abyssinian maid,
   And on her dulcimer she played,
   Singing of Mount Abora.
   Could I revive within me
   Her symphony and song,
     To such a deep delight 'twould win me,
That with music loud and long,
I would build that dome in air,
That sunny dome! those caves of ice!
And all who heard should see them there,
And all should cry, Beware! Beware!
His flashing eyes, his floating hair!
Weave a circle round him thrice,
And close your eyes with holy dread,
For he on honey-dew hath fed,
And drunk the milk of Paradise.

Samuel Taylor Coleridge 57

Christabel

[PART 1, 1797; PART II, 1800; THE CONCLUSION TO PART II, 1801]

The first part of the following poem was written in the year one thousand seven hundred and ninety seven, at Stowey, in the county of Somerset. The second part, after my return from Germany, in the year one thousand eight hundred, at Keswick, Cumberland. [Since the latter date, my poetic powers have been, till very lately, in a state of suspended animation. But as, in my very first conception of the tale, I had the whole present to my mind, with the wholeness, no less than the liveliness of a vision; I trust that I shall be able to embody in verse the three parts yet to come, in the course of the present year.—These sentences omitted in 1834 edition.] It is probable that if the poem had been finished at either of the former periods, or if even the first and second part had been published in the year 1800, the impression of its originality would have been much greater than I dare at present expect. But for this I have only my own indolence to blame. The dates are mentioned for the exclusive purpose of precluding charges of plagiarism or servile imitation from myself. For there is amongst us a set of critics, who seem to hold, that every possible thought and image is traditional; who have no notion that there are such things as fountains in the world, small as well as great; and who would therefore charitably derive every rill they behold flowing, from a perforation made in some other man's tank. I am confident, however, that as far as the present poem is concerned, the celebrated poets [Sir Walter Scott & Lord Byron] whose writings I might be suspected of having imitated, either in particular passages, or in the tone and the spirit of the whole, would be among the first to vindicate me from the charge, and who, on any striking coincidence, would permit me to address them in this doggerel version of two monkish Latin hexameters.

> 'Tis mine and it is likewise yours;
> But an if this will not do;
> Let it be mine, good friend! for I
> Am the poorer of the two.

I have only to add that the metre of Christabel is not, properly speaking, irregular, though it may seem so from its being founded on a new principle: namely, that of counting in each line the accents, not the syllables. Though the latter may vary from seven [actually, four] to twelve, yet in each line the accents will be found to be only four. Nevertheless, this occasional variation in number of syllables is not introduced wantonly, or for the mere ends of convenience, but in correspondence with some transition in the nature of the imagery or passion.

Part I

'Tis the middle of night by the castle clock,
And the owls have awakened the crowing cock;
Tu—whit!——Tu—whoo!
And hark, again! the crowing cock,
How drowsily it crew.
Sir Leoline, the Baron rich,
Hath a toothless mastiff bitch;
From her kennel beneath the rock
She maketh answer to the clock,
Four for the quarters, and twelve for the hour;
Ever and aye, by shine and shower,
Sixteen short howls, not over loud;
Some say, she sees my lady's shroud.

Is the night chilly and dark?
The night is chilly, but not dark.
The thin gray cloud is spread on high,
It covers but not hides the sky.
The moon is behind, and at the full;
And yet she looks both small and dull.
The night is chill, the cloud is gray:
'Tis a month before the month of May,
And the Spring comes slowly up this way.

The lovely lady, Christabel,
Whom her father loves so well,
What makes her in the wood so late,
A furlong from the castle gate?
She had dreams all yesternight
Of her own betrothéd knight;
And she in the midnight wood will pray
For the weal of her lover that's far away.

She stole along, she nothing spoke,
The sighs she heaved were soft and low,
And naught was green upon the oak
But moss and rarest misletoe:
She kneels beneath the huge oak tree,
And in silence prayeth she.

The lady sprang up suddenly,
The lovely lady, Christabel!
It moaned as near, as near can be,
But what it is she cannot tell.—
On the other side it seems to be,
Of the huge, broad-breasted, old oak tree.

The night is chill; the forest bare;
Is it the wind that moaneth bleak?
There is not wind enough in the air
To move away the ringlet curl
From the lovely lady's cheek—
There is not wind enough to twirl
The one red leaf, the last of its clan,
That dances as often as dance it can,
Hanging so light, and hanging so high,
On the topmost twig that looks up at the sky.

Hush, beating heart of Christabel!
Jesu, Maria, shield her well!
She folded her arms beneath her cloak,
And stole to the other side of the oak.
      What sees she there?

There she sees a damsel bright,
Dressed in a silken robe of white,
That shadowy in the moonlight shone:
The neck that made that white robe wan,
Her stately neck, and arms were bare;
Her blue-veined feet unsandal'd were;
And wildly glittered here and there
The gems entangled in her hair.
I guess, 'twas frightful there to see
A lady so richly clad as she—
Beautiful exceedingly!

Mary mother, save me now!
(Said Christabel,) And who art thou?

The lady strange made answer meet,
And her voice was faint and sweet:—
Have pity on my sore distress,
I scarce can speak for weariness:
Stretch forth thy hand, and have no fear!

Said Christabel, How camest thou here?
And the lady, whose voice was faint and sweet,
Did thus pursue her answer meet:—

My sire is of a noble line,
And my name is Geraldine:
Five warriors seized me yestermorn,
Me, even me, a maid forlorn:
They choked my cries with force and fright,
And tied me on a palfrey white.
The palfrey was as fleet as wind,
And they rode furiously behind.

They spurred amain, their steeds were white:
And once we crossed the shade of night.
As sure as Heaven shall rescue me,
I have no thought what men they be;
Nor do I know how long it is
(For I have lain entranced, I wis)
Since one, the tallest of the five,
Took me from the palfrey's back,
A weary woman, scarce alive.
Some muttered words his comrades spoke:
He placed me underneath this oak;
He swore they would return with haste;
Whither they went I cannot tell—
I thought I heard, some minutes past,
Sounds as of a castle bell.
Stretch forth thy hand (thus ended she),
And help a wretched maid to flee.

Then Christabel stretched forth her hand,
And comforted fair Geraldine:
O well, bright dame! may you command
The service of Sir Leoline;
And gladly our stout chivalry
Will he send forth and friends withal
To guide and guard you safe and free
Home to your noble father's hall.

She rose: and forth with steps they passed
That strove to be, and were not, fast.
Her gracious stars the lady blest,
And thus spake on sweet Christabel:
All our household are at rest,

The hall is silent as the cell;
Sir Leoline is weak in health,
And may not well awakened be,
But we will move as if in stealth,
And I beseech your courtesy,
This night, to share your couch with me.

They crossed the moat, and Christabel
Took the key that fitted well;
A little door she opened straight,
All in the middle of the gate;
The gate that was ironed within and without,
Where an army in battle array had marched out.
The lady sank, belike through pain,
And Christabel with might and main
Lifted her up, a weary weight,
Over the threshold of the gate:
Then the lady rose again,
And moved, as she were not in pain.

So free from danger, free from fear,
They crossed the court: right glad they were.
And Christabel devoutly cried
To the Lady by her side,
Praise we the Virgin all divine
Who hath rescued thee from thy distress!
Alas, alas! said Geraldine,
I cannot speak for weariness.
So free from danger, free from fear,
They crossed the court: right glad they were.

Outside her kennel, the mastiff old
Lay fast asleep, in moonshine cold.
The mastiff old did not awake,
Yet she an angry moan did make!
And what can ail the mastiff bitch?
Never till now she uttered yell
Beneath the eye of Christabel.
Perhaps it is the owlet's scritch:
For what can aid the mastiff bitch?

They passed the hall, that echoes still,
Pass as lightly as you will!
The brands were flat, the brands were dying,
Amid their own white ashes lying;

But when the lady passed, there came
A tongue of light, a fit of flame;
And Christabel saw the lady's eye,
And nothing else saw she thereby,
Save the boss of the shield of Sir Leoline tall,
Which hung in a murky old niche in the wall.
O softly tread, said Christabel,
My father seldom sleepeth well.

Sweet Christabel her feet doth bare,
And jealous of the listening air
They steal their way from stair to stair,
Now in glimmer, and now in gloom,
And now they pass the Baron's room,
As still as death, with stifled breath!
And now have reached her chamber door;
And now doth Geraldine press down
The rushes of the chamber floor.

The moon shines dim in the open air,
And not a moonbeam enters here.
But they without its light can see
The chamber carved so curiously,
Carved with figures strange and sweet,
All made out of the carver's brain,
For a lady's chamber meet:
The lamp with twofold silver chain
Is fastened to an angel's feet.

The silver lamp burns dead and dim;
But Christabel the lamp will trim.
She trimmed the lamp, and made it bright,
And left it swinging to and fro,
While Geraldine, in wretched plight,
Sank down upon the floor below.

O weary lady, Geraldine,
I pray you, drink this cordial wine!
It is a wine of virtuous powers;
My mother made it of wild flowers.

And will your mother pity me,
Who am a maiden most forlorn?
Christabel answered—Woe is me!
She died the hour that I was born.

I have heard the gray-haired friar tell
How on her death-bed she did say,
That she should hear the castle-bell
Strike twelve upon my wedding-day.
O mother dear! that thou wert here!
I would, said Geraldine, she were!

But soon with altered voice, said she—
'Off, wandering mother! Peak and pine!
I have power to bid thee flee.'
Alas! what ails poor Geraldine?
Why stares she with unsettled eye?
Can she the bodiless dead espy?
And why with hollow voice cries she,
'Off, woman, off! this hour is mine—
Though thou her guardian spirit be,
Off, woman. off! 'tis given to me.'

Then Christabel knelt by the lady's side,
And raised to heaven her eyes so blue—
Alas! said she, this ghastly ride—
Dear lady! it hath wildered you!
The lady wiped her moist cold brow,
And faintly said, ''Tis over now!'

Again the wild-flower wine she drank:
Her fair large eyes 'gan glitter bright,
And from the floor whereon she sank,
The lofty lady stood upright:
She was most beautiful to see,
Like a lady of a far countrée.

And thus the lofty lady spake—
'All they who live in the upper sky,
Do love you, holy Christabel!
And you love them, and for their sake
And for the good which me befel,
Even I in my degree will try,
Fair maiden, to requite you well.
But now unrobe yourself; for I
Must pray, ere yet in bed I lie.'

Quoth Christabel, So let it be!
And as the lady bade, did she.
Her gentle limbs did she undress
And lay down in her loveliness.

But through her brain of weal and woe
So many thoughts moved to and fro,
That vain it were her lids to close;
So half-way from the bed she rose,
And on her elbow did recline
To look at the lady Geraldine.

Beneath the lamp the lady bowed,
And slowly rolled her eyes around;
Then drawing in her breath aloud,
Like one that shuddered, she unbound
The cincture from beneath her breast:
Her silken robe, and inner vest,
Dropt to her feet, and full in view,
Behold! her bosom, and half her side——
A sight to dream of, not to tell!
O shield her! shield sweet Christabel!

Yet Geraldine nor speaks nor stirs;
Ah! what a stricken look was hers!
Deep from within she seems half-way
To lift some weight with sick assay,
And eyes the maid and seeks delay;
Then suddenly as one defied
Collects herself in scorn and pride,
And lay down by the Maiden's side!—
And in her arms the maid she took,
      Ah wel-a-day!
And with low voice and doleful look
These words did say:
'In the touch of this bosom there worketh a spell,
Which is lord of thy utterance, Christabel!
Thou knowest to-night, and wilt know to-morrow
This mark of my shame, this seal of my sorrow;
      But vainly thou warrest,
        For this is alone in
      Thy power to declare,
        That in the dim forest
      Thou heard'st a low moaning,

The death-note to their living brother;
And oft too, by the knell offended,
Just as their one! two! three! is ended,
The devil mocks the doleful tale
With a merry peal from Borodale.

The air is still! through mist and cloud
That merry peal comes ringing loud;
And Geraldine shakes off her dread,
And rises lightly from the bed;
Puts on her silken vestments white,
And tricks her hair in lovely plight,
And nothing doubting of her spell
Awakens the lady Christabel.
'Sleep you, sweet lady Christabel?
I trust that you have rested well.'

And Christabel awoke and spied
The same who lay down by her side—
O rather say, the same whom she
Raised up beneath the old oak tree!
Nay, fairer yet! and yet more fair!
For she belike hath drunken deep
Of all the blessedness of sleep!
And while she spake, her looks, her air
Such gentle thankfulness declare,
That (so it seemed) her girded vests
Grew tight beneath her heaving breasts.
'Sure I have sinn'd!' said Christabel,
'Now heaven be praised if all be well!'
And in low faltering tones, yet sweet,
Did she the lofty lady greet
With such perplexity of mind
As dreams too lively leave behind.

So quickly she rose, and quickly arrayed
Her maiden limbs, and having prayed
That He, who on the cross did groan,
Might wash away her sins unknown,
She forthwith led fair Geraldine
To meet her sire, Sir Leoline.

The lovely maid and the lady tall
Are pacing both into the hall,
And pacing on through page and groom,
Enter the Baron's presence-room.

The Baron rose, and while he prest
His gentle daughter to his breast,
With cheerful wonder in his eyes
The lady Geraldine espies,
And gave such welcome to the same,
As might beseem so bright a dame!

But when he heard the lady's tale,
And when she told her father's name,
Why waxed Sir Leoline so pale,
Murmuring o'er the name again,
Lord Roland de Vaux of Tryermaine?

Alas! they had been friends in youth;
But whispering tongues can poison truth;
And constancy lives in realms above;
And life is thorny; and youth is vain;
And to be wroth with one we love,
Doth work like madness in the brain.
And thus it chanced, as I divine,
With Roland and Sir Leoline.
Each spake words of high disdain
And insult to his heart's best brother:
They parted—ne'er to meet again!
But never either found another
To free the hollow heart from paining—
They stood aloof, the scars remaining,
Like cliffs which had been rent asunder;
A dreary sea now flows between;—
But neither heat, nor frost, nor thunder,
Shall wholly do away, I ween,
The marks of that which once hath been.

Sir Leoline, a moment's space,
Stood gazing on the damsel's face:
And the youthful Lord of Tryermaine
Came back upon his heart again.

O then the Baron forgot his age,
His noble heart swelled high with rage;
He swore by the wounds in Jesu's side,
He would proclaim it far and wide
With trump and solemn heraldry,
That they, who thus had wronged the dame,
Were base as spotted infamy!
'And if they dare deny the same,
My herald shall appoint a week,
And let the recreant traitors seek
My tourney court—that there and then
I may dislodge their reptile souls
From the bodies and forms of men!'
He spake: his eye in lightning rolls!
For the lady was ruthlessly seized; and he kenned
In the beautiful lady the child of his friend!
And now the tears were on his face,
And fondly in his arms he took
Fair Geraldine, who met the embrace,
Prolonging it with joyous look.
Which when she viewed, a vision fell
Upon the soul of Christabel,
The vision of fear, the touch and pain!
She shrunk and shuddered, and saw again—
(Ah, woe is me! Was it for thee,
Thou gentle maid! such sights to see?)

Again she saw that bosom old,
Again she felt that bosom cold,
And drew in her breath with a hissing sound:
Whereat the Knight turned wildly round,
And nothing saw, but his own sweet maid
With eyes upraised, as one that prayed.

The touch, the sight, had passed away,
And in its stead that vision blest,
Which comforted her after-rest.
While in the lady's arms she lay,
Had put a rapture in her breast,
And on her lips and o'er her eyes
Spread smiles like light!
                With new surprise,
'What ails then my belovéd child?'
The Baron said—His daughter mild

Made answer, 'All will yet be well!'
I ween, she had no power to tell
Aught else: so mighty was the spell.

Yet he, who saw this Geraldine,
Had deemed her sure a thing divine:
Such sorrow with such grace she blended,
As if she feared she had offended
Sweet Christabel, that gentle maid!
And with such lowly tones she prayed,
She might be sent without delay
Home to her father's mansion.
                              'Nay!
Nay, by my soul!' said Leoline.
'Ho! Bracy the bard, the charge be thine!
Go thou, with music sweet and loud,
And take two steeds with trappings proud,
And take the youth whom thou lov'st best
To bear thy harp, and learn thy song,
And clothe you both in solemn vest,
And over the mountains haste along,
Lest wandering folk, that are abroad,
Detain you on the valley road.

'And when he has crossed the Irthing flood,
My merry bard! he hastes, he hastes
Up Knorren Moor, through Halegarth Wood,
And reaches soon that castle good
Which stands and threatens Scotland's wastes.

'Bard Bracy! bard Bracy! your horses are fleet,
Ye must ride up the hall, your music so sweet,
More loud than your horses' echoing feet!
And loud and loud to Lord Roland call,
Thy daughter is safe in Langdale hall!
Thy beautiful daughter is safe and free—
Sir Leoline greets thee thus through me!
He bids thee come without delay
With all thy numerous array
And take thy lovely daughter home:
And he will meet thee on the way
With all his numerous array
White with their panting palfreys' foam:
And, by mine honour! I will say,
That I repent me of the day

When I spake words of fierce disdain
To Roland de Vaux of Tryermaine!—
—For since that evil hour hath flown,
Many a summer's sun hath shone;
Yet ne'er found I a friend again
Like Roland de Vaux of Tryermaine.'

The lady fell, and clasped his knees,
Her face upraised, her eyes o'erflowing;
And Bracy replied, with faltering voice,
His gracious hail on all bestowing!—
'Thy words, thou sire of Christabel,
Are sweeter than my harp can tell;
Yet might I gain a boon of thee,
This day my journey should not be,
So strange a dream hath come to me,
That I had vowed with music loud
To clear yon wood from thing unblest,
Warned by a vision in my rest!
For in my sleep I saw that dove,
That gentle bird, whom thou dost love,
And call'st by thy own daughter's name—
Sir Leoline! I saw the same
Fluttering, and uttering fearful moan,
Among the green herbs in the forest alone.
Which when I saw and when I heard,
I wonder'd what might ail the bird;
For nothing near it could I see,
Save the grass and herbs underneath the old tree.

'And in my dream methought I went
To search out what might there be found;
And what the sweet bird's trouble meant,
That thus lay fluttering on the ground.
I went and peered, and could descry
No cause for her distressful cry;
But yet for her dear lady's sake
I stooped, methought, the dove to take,
When lo! I saw a bright green snake
Coiled around its wings and neck.
Green as the herbs on which it couched,
Close by the dove's its head it crouched;
And with the dove it heaves and stirs,
Swelling its neck as she swelled hers!
I woke; it was the midnight hour,

The clock was echoing in the tower;
But though my slumber was gone by,
This dream it would not pass away—
It seems to live upon my eye!
And thence I vowed this self-same day,
With music strong and saintly song
To wander through the forest bare,
Lest aught unholy loiter there.'

Thus Bracy said: the Baron, the while,
Half-listening heard him with a smile;
Then turned to Lady Geraldine,
His eyes made up of wonder and love;
And said in courtly accents fine,
'Sweet maid, Lord Roland's beauteous dove,
With arms more strong than harp or song,
Thy sire and I will crush the snake!'
He kissed her forehead as he spake,
And Geraldine in maiden wise,
Casting down her large bright eyes,
With blushing cheek and courtesy fine
She turned her from Sir Leoline;
Softly gathering up her train,
That o'er her right arm fell again;
And folded her arms across her chest,
And couched her head upon her breast,
And looked askance at Christabel——
Jesu, Maria, shield her well!

A snake's small eye blinks dull and shy;
And the lady's eyes they shrunk in her head,
Each shrunk up to a serpent's eye,
And with somewhat of malice, and more of dread,
At Christabel she looked askance!—
One moment—and the sight was fled!
But Christabel in dizzy trance
Stumbling on the unsteady ground
Shuddered aloud, with a hissing sound;
And Geraldine again turned round,
And like a thing, that sought relief,
Full of wonder and full of grief,
She rolled her large bright eyes divine
Wildly on Sir Leoline.

The maid, alas! her thoughts are gone,
She nothing sees—no sight but one!
The maid, devoid of guile and sin,
I know not how, in fearful wise,
So deeply had she drunken in
That look, those shrunken serpent eyes,
That all her features were resigned
To this sole image in her mind:
And passively did imitate
That look of dull and treacherous hate!
And thus she stood, in dizzy trance,
Still picturing that look askance
With forced unconscious sympathy
Full before her father's view——
As far as such a look could be
In eyes so innocent and blue!

And when the trance was o'er, the maid
Paused awhile, and inly prayed:
Then falling at the Baron's feet,
'By my mother's soul do I entreat
That thou this woman send away!'
She said: and more she could not say:
For what she knew she could not tell,
O'er-mastered by the mighty spell.

Why is thy cheek so wan and wild,
Sir Leoline? Thy only child
Lies at thy feet, thy joy, thy pride,
So fair, so innocent, so mild;
The same, for whom thy lady died!
O by the pangs of her dear mother
Think thou no evil of thy child!
For her, and thee, and for no other,
She prayed the moment ere she died:
Prayed that the babe for whom she died,
Might prove her dear lord's joy and pride!
    That prayer her deadly pangs beguiled,
        Sir Leoline!
    And wouldst thou wrong thy only child,
        Her child and thine?
Within the Baron's heart and brain
If thoughts, like these, had any share,
They only swelled his rage and pain,

And did but work confusion there.
His heart was cleft with pain and rage,
His cheeks they quivered, his eyes were wild,
Dishonored thus in his old age;
Dishonored by his only child,
And all his hospitality
To the wronged daughter of his friend
By more than woman's jealousy
Brought thus to a disgraceful end—
He rolled his eye with stern regard
Upon the gentle minstrel bard,
And said in tones abrupt, austere—
'Why, Bracy! dost thou loiter here?
I bade thee hence!' The bard obeyed;
And turning from his own sweet maid,
The agéd knight, Sir Leoline,
Led forth the lady Geraldine!

The Conclusion to Part II

A little child, a limber elf,
Singing, dancing to itself,
A fairy thing with red round cheeks,
That always finds, and never seeks,
Makes such a vision to the sight
As fills a father's eyes with light;
And pleasures flow in so thick and fast
Upon his heart, that he at last
Must needs express his love's excess
With words of unmeant bitterness.
Perhaps 'tis pretty to force together
Thoughts so all unlike each other;
To mutter and mock a broken charm,
To dally with wrong that does no harm.
Perhaps 'tis tender too and pretty
At each wild word to feel within
A sweet recoil of love and pity.
And what, if in a world of sin
(O sorrow and shame should this be true!)
Such giddiness of heart and brain
Comes seldom save from rage and pain,
So talks as it's most used to do.

Samuel Taylor Coleridge

The Eolian Harp

[1795]

My pensive Sara! thy soft cheek reclined
Thus on mine arm, most soothing sweet it is
To sit beside our Cot, our Cot o'ergrown
With white-flower'd Jasmin, and the broad-leav'd Myrtle,
(Meet emblems they of Innocence and Love!)
And watch the clouds, that late were rich with light,
Slow saddenning round, and mark the star of eve
Serenely brilliant (such should Wisdom be)
Shine opposite! How exquisite the scents
Snatch'd from yon bean-field! and the world so hush'd!
The stilly murmur of the distant Sea
Tells us of silence.
                And that simplest Lute,
Placed length-ways in the clasping casement, hark!
How by the desultory breeze caress'd,
Like some coy maid half-yielding to her lover,
It pours such sweet upbraiding, as must needs
Tempt to repeat the wrong! And now, its strings
Boldlier swept, the long sequacious notes
Over delicious surges sink and rise,
Such a soft floating witchery of sound
As twilight Elfins make, when they at eve
Voyage on gentle gales from Fairy-Land,
Where Melodies round honey-dropping flowers,
Footless and wild, like birds of Paradise,
Nor pause, nor perch, hovering on untam'd wing!
O! the one Life within us and abroad,
Which meets all motion and becomes its soul,
A light in sound, a sound-like power in light,
Rhythm in all thought, and joyance every where—
Methinks, it should have been impossible
Not to love all things in a world so fill'd;
Where the breeze warbles, and the mute still air
Is Music slumbering on her instrument.

   And thus, my Love! as on the midway slope
Of yonder hill I stretch my limbs at noon,
Whilst thro' my half-clos'd eye-lids I behold
The sunbeams dance, like diamonds, on the main,
And tranquil muse upon tranquility;

Full many a thought uncall'd and undetain'd,
And many idle flitting phantasies,
Traverse my indolent and passive brain,
As wild and various, as the random gales
That swell and flutter on this subject Lute!

   And what if all of animated nature
Be but organic Harps diversly fram'd,
That tremble into thought, as o'er them sweeps
Plastic and vast, one intellectual breeze,
At once the Soul of each, and God of all?

   But thy more serious eye a mild reproof
Darts, O belovéd Woman! nor such thoughts
Dim and unhallow'd dost thou not reject,
And biddest me walk humbly with my God.
Meek Daughter in the Family of Christ!
Well hast thou said and holily disprais'd
These shapings of the unregenerate mind;
Bubbles that glitter as they rise and break
On vain Philosophy's aye-babbling spring.
For never guiltless may I speak of him,
The Incomprehensible! save when with awe
I praise him, and with Faith that inly feels;
Who with his saving mercies healéd me,
A sinful and most miserable man,
Wilder'd and dark, and gave me to possess
Peace, and this Cot, and thee, heart-honour'd Maid!

Reflections on Having Left a Place of Retirement

[1795]

Sermoni propriora.—HORACE

Low was our pretty Cot: our tallest Rose
Peep'd at the chamber-window. We could hear
At silent noon, and eve, and early morn,
The Sea's faint murmur. In the open air
Our Myrtles blossom'd; and across the porch
Thick Jasmins twined: the little landscape round
Was green and woody, and refresh'd the eye.
It was a spot which you might aptly call
The Valley of Seclusion! Once I saw
(Hallowing his Sabbath-day by quiteness)

A wealthy son of Commerce saunter by,
Bristowa's citizen: methought, it calm'd
His thirst of idle gold, and made him muse
With wiser feelings: for he paus'd, and look'd
With a pleas'd sadness, and gaz'd all around,
Then eyed our Cottage, and gaz'd round again,
And sigh'd, and said, it was a Blessèd Place.
And we were bless'd. Oft with patient ear
Long-listening to the viewless sky-lark's note
(Viewless, or haply for a moment seen
Gleaming on sunny wings) in whisper'd tones
I said to my Belovéd, 'Such, sweet Girl!
The inobtrusive song of Happiness,
Unearthly minstrelsy! then only heard
When the Soul seeks to hear; when all is hush'd,
And the Heart listens!'

                  But the time, when first
From that low Dell, steep up the stony Mount
I climb'd with perilous toil and reach'd the top,
Oh! what a goodly scene! Here the bleak mount,
The bare bleak mountain speckled thin with sheep;
Grey clouds, that shadowing spot the sunny fields;
And river, now with bushy rocks o'er-brow'd,
Now winding bright and full, with naked banks;
And seats, and lawns, the Abbey and the wood,
And cots, and hamlets, and faint city-spire;
The Channel there, the Islands and white sails,
Dim coasts, and cloud-like hills, and shoreless Ocean—
It seem'd like Omnipresence! God, methought,
Had build him there a Temple: the whole World
Seem'd imag'd in its vast circumference:
No wish profan'd my overwhelmèd heart.
Blest hour! It was a luxury,—to be!

    Ah! quiet Dell! dear Cot, and Mount sublime!
I was constrain'd to quit you. Was it right,
While my unnumber'd brethren toil'd and bled,
That I should dream away the entrusted hours
On rose-leaf beds, pampering the coward heart
With feelings all too delicate for use?
Sweet is the tear that from some Howard's eye
Drops on the cheek of one he lifts from earth:
And he that works me good with unmov'd face,
Does it but half: he chills me while he aids,

My benefactor, not my brother man!
Yet even this, this cold beneficience
Praise, praise it, O my Soul! oft as thou scann'st
The sluggard Pity's vision-weaving tribe!
Who sigh for Wretchedness, yet shun the Wretched,
Nursing in some delicious solitude
Their slothful loves and dainty sympathies!
I therefore go, and join head, heart, and hand,
Active and firm, to fight the bloodless fight
Of Science, Freedom, and the Truth in Christ.

Yet oft when after honourable toil
Rests the tir'd mind, and waking loves to dream,
My spirit shall revisit thee, dear Cot!
Thy Jasmin and thy window-peeping Rose,
And Myrtles fearless of the mild sea-air.
And I shall sigh fond wishes—sweet Abode!
Ah!—had none greater! And that all had such!
It might be so—but the time is not yet.
Speed it, O Father! Let thy Kingdom come!

This Lime-Tree Bower My Prison

[1797]

ADDRESSED TO CHARLES LAMB, OF THE INDIA HOUSE, LONDON

In the June of 1797 some long-expected Friends [William & Dorothy Wordsworth and Charles Lamb] paid a visit to the author's cottage; and on the morning of their arrival, he met with an accident [his wife spilled a skillet of boiling milk on his foot], which disabled him from walking during the whole time of their stay. One evening, when they had left him for a few hours, he composed the following lines in the garden-bower.

Well, they are gone, and here must I remain,
This lime-tree bower my prison! I have lost
Beauties and feelings, such as would have been
Most sweet to my remembrance even when age
Had dimm'd mine eyes to blindness! They, meanwhile,
Friends, whom I never more may meet again,
On springy heath, along the hill-top edge,
Wander in gladness, and wind down, perchance,
To that still roaring dell, of which I told;
The roaring dell, o'erwooded, narrow, deep,

And only speckled by the mid-day sun;
Where its slim trunk the ash from rock to rock
Flings arching like a bridge;—that branchless ash,
Unsunn'd and damp, whose few poor yellow leaves
Ne'er tremble in the gale, yet tremble still,
Fann'd by the water-fall! and there my friends
Behold the dark green file of long lank weeds,
That all at once (a most fantastic sight!)
Still nod and drip beneath the dripping edge
Of the blue clay-stone.

          Now, my friends emerge
Beneath the wide wide Heaven—and view again
The many-steepled tract magnificent
Of hilly fields and meadows, and the sea,
With some fair bark, perhaps, whose sails light up
The slip of smooth clear blue betwixt two Isles
Of purple shadow! Yes! they wander on
In gladness all; but thou, methinks, most glad,
My gentle-hearted Charles! for thou hast pined
And hunger'd after Nature, many a year,
In the great City pent, winning thy way
With sad yet patient soul, through evil and pain
And strange calamity! Ah! slowly sink
Behind the western ridge, thou glorious Sun!
Shine in the slant beams of the sinking orb,
Ye purple heath-flowers! richlier burn, ye clouds!
Live in the yellow light, ye distant groves!
And kindle, thou blue Ocean! So my friend
Struck with deep joy may stand, as I have stood,
Silent with swimming sense; yea, gazing round
On the wide landscape, gaze till all doth seem
Less gross than bodily; and of such hues
As veil the Almighty Spirit, when yet he makes
Spirits perceive his presence.

          A delight
Comes sudden on my heart, and I am glad
As I myself were there! Nor in this bower,
This little lime-tree bower, have I not mark'd
Much that has sooth'd me. Pale beneath the blaze
Hung the transparent foliage; and I watch'd
Some broad and sunny leaf, and lov'd to see
The shadow of the leaf and stem above
Dappling its sunshine! And that walnut-tree

Was richly ting'd, and a deep radiance lay
Full on the ancient ivy, which usurps
Those fronting elms, and now, with blackest mass
Makes their dark branches gleam a lighter hue
Through the late twilight: and though now the bat
Wheels silent by, and not a swallow twitters,
Yet still the solitary humble-bee
Sings in the bean-flower! Henceforth I shall know
That Nature ne'er deserts the wise and pure;
No plot so narrow, be but Nature there,
No waste so vacant, but may well employ
Each faculty of sense, and keep the heart
Awake to Love and Beauty! and sometimes
'Tis well to be bereft of promis'd good,
That we may lift the soul, and contemplate
With lively joy the joys we cannot share.
My gentle-hearted Charles! when the last rook
Beat its straight path across the dusky air
Homewards, I blest it! deeming its black wing
(Now a dim speck, now vanishing in light)
Had cross'd the mighty Orb's dilated glory,
While thou stood'st gazing; or, when all was still,
Flew creeking o'er thy head, and had a charm
For thee, my gentle-hearted Charles, to whom
No sound is dissonant which tells of Life.

Frost at Midnight

[1798]

The Frost performs its secret ministry,
Unhelped by any wind. The owlet's cry
Came loud—and hark, again! loud as before.
The inmates of my cottage, all at rest,
Have left me to that solitude, which suits
Abstruser musings: save that at my side
My cradled infant slumbers peacefully.
'Tis calm indeed! so calm, that it disturbs
And vexes meditation with its strange
And extreme silentness. Sea, hill, and wood,
This populous village! Sea, and hill, and wood,
With all the numberless goings-on of life,
Inaudible as dreams! the thin blue flame
Lies on my low-burnt fire, and quivers not;
Only that film, which fluttered on the grate,

Still flutters there, the sole unquiet thing.
Methinks, its motion in this hush of nature
Gives it dim sympathies with me who live,
Making it a companionable form,
Whose puny flaps and freaks the idling Spirit
By its own moods interprets, every where
Echo or mirror seeking of itself,
And makes a toy of Thought.

                              But O! how oft,
How oft, at school, with most believing mind,
Presageful, have I gazed upon the bars,
To watch that fluttering stranger! and as oft
With unclosed lids, already had I dreamt
Of my sweet birth-place, and the old church-tower,
Whose bells, the poor man's only music, rang
From morn to evening, all the hot Fair-day,
So sweetly, that they stirred and haunted me
With a wild pleasure, falling on mine ear
Most like articulate sounds of things to come!
So gazed I, till the soothing things, I dreamt,
Lulled me to sleep, and sleep prolonged my dreams!
And so I brooded all the following morn,
Awed by the stern preceptor's face, mine eye
Fixed with mock study on my swimming book:
Save if the door half opened, and I snatched
A hasty glance, and still my heart leaped up,
For still I hoped to see the stranger's face,
Townsman, or aunt, or sister more beloved,
My play-mate when we both were clothed alike!

   Dear Babe, that sleepest cradled by my side,
Whose gentle breathings, heard in this deep calm,
Fill up the interspersèd vacancies
And momentary pauses of the thought!
My babe so beautiful! it thrills my heart
With tender gladness, thus to look at thee,
And think that thou shalt learn far other lore,
And in far other scenes! For I was reared
In the great city, pent 'mid cloisters dim,
And saw nought lovely but the sky and stars.
But thou, my babe! shalt wander like a breeze
By lakes and sandy shores, beneath the crags
Of ancient mountain, and beneath the clouds,
Which image in their bulk both lakes and shores

And mountain crags: so shalt thou see and hear
The lovely shapes and sounds intelligible
Of that eternal language, which thy God
Utters, who from eternity doth teach
Himself in all, and all things in himself.
Great universal Teacher! he shall mould
Thy spirit, and by giving make it ask.

  Therefore all seasons shall be sweet to thee,
Whether the summer clothe the general earth
With greenness, or the redbreast sit and sing
Betwixt the tufts of snow on the bare branch
Of mossy apple-tree, while the nigh thatch
Smokes in the sun-thaw; whether the eave-drops fall
Heard only in the trances of the blast,
Or if the secret ministry of frost
Shall hang them up in silent icicles,
Quietly shining to the quiet Moon.

Fears in Solitude

[1798]

WRITTEN IN APRIL 1798, DURING THE ALARM OF AN INVASION

A green and silent spot, amid the hills,
A small and silent dell! O'er stiller place
No singing sky-lark ever poised himself.
The hills are heathy, save that swelling slope,
Which hath a gay and gorgeous covering on,
All golden with the never-bloomless furze,
Which now blooms most profusely: but the dell,
Bathed by the mist, is fresh and delicate
As vernal corn-field, or the unripe flax,
When, through its half-transparent stalks, at eve,
The level sunshine glimmers with green light.
Oh! 'tis a quiet spirit-healing nook!
Which all, methinks, would love; but chiefly he,
The humble man, who, in his youthful years,
Knew just so much of folly, as had made
His early manhood more securely wise!
Here he might lie on fern or withered heath,
While from the singing lark (that sings unseen
The minstrelsy that solitude loves best),
And from the sun, and from the breezy air,

Sweet influences trembled o'er his frame;
And he, with many feelings, many thoughts,
Made up a meditative joy, and found
Religious meanings in the forms of Nature!
And so, his senses gradually wrapt
In a half sleep, he dreams of better worlds,
And dreaming hears thee still, O singing lark,
That singest like an angel in the clouds!

   My God! it is a melancholy thing
For such a man, who would full fain preserve
His soul in calmness, yet perforce must feel
For all his human brethren—O my God!
It weighs upon the heart, that he must think
What uproar and what strife may now be stirring
This way or that way o'er these silent hills—
Invasion, and the thunder and the shout,
And all the crash of onset; fear and rage,
And undetermined conflict—even now,
Even now, perchance, and in his native isle:
Carnage and groans beneath this blessed sun!
We have offended, Oh! my countrymen!
We have offended very grievously,
And been most tyrannous. From east to west
A groan of accusation pierces Heaven!
The wretched plead against us; multitudes
Countless and vehement, the sons of God,
Our brethren! Like a cloud that travels on,
Steamed up from Cairo's swamps of pestilence,
Even so, my countrymen! have we gone forth
And borne to distant tribes slavery and pangs,
And, deadlier far, our vices, whose deep taint
With slow perdition murders the whole man,
His body and his soul! Meanwhile, at home,
All individual dignity and power
Engulfed in Courts, Committees, Institutions,
Associations and Societies,
A vain, speech-mouthing, speech-reporting Guild,
One Benefit-Club for mutual flattery,
We have drunk up, demure as at a grace,
Pollutions from the brimming cup of wealth;
Contemptuous of all honourable rule,
Yet bartering freedom and the poor man's life
For gold, as at a market! The sweet words
Of Christian promise, words that even yet

Might stem destruction, were they wisely preached,
Are muttered o'er by men, whose tones proclaim
How flat and wearisome they feel their trade:
Rank scoffers some, but most too indolent
To deem them falsehoods or to know their truth.
Oh! blasphemous! the Book of Life is made
A superstitious instrument, on which
We gabble o'er the oaths we mean to break;
For all must swear—all and in every place,
College and wharf, council and justice-court;
All, all must swear, the briber and the bribed,
Merchant and lawyer, senator and priest,
The rich, the poor, the old man and the young;
All, all make up one scheme of perjury,
That faith doth reel; the very name of God
Sounds like a juggler's charm; and, bold with joy,
Forth from his dark and lonely hiding-place,
(Portentous sight!) the owlet Atheism,
Sailing on obscene wings athwart the noon,
Drops his blue-fringéd lids, and holds them close,
And hooting at the glorious sun in Heaven,
Cries out, 'Where is it?'

       Thankless too for peace,
(Peace long preserved by fleets and perilous seas)
Secure from actual warfare, we have loved
To swell the war-whoop, passionate for war!
Alas! for ages ignorant of all
Its ghastlier workings, (famine or blue plague,
Battle, or siege, or flight through wintry snows,)
We, this whole people, have been clamorous
For war and bloodshed; animating sports,
The which we pay for as a thing to talk of,
Spectators and not combatants! No guess
Anticipative of a wrong unfelt,
No speculation on contingency,
However dim and vague, too vague and dim
To yield a justifying cause; and forth,
(Stuffed out with big preamble, holy names,
And adjurations of the God in Heaven,)
We send our mandates for the certain death
Of thousands and ten thousands! Boys and girls,
And women, that would groan to see a child
Pull off an insect's wing, all read of war,
The best amusement for our morning meal!

The poor wretch, who has learnt his only prayers
From curses, and who knows scarcely words enough
To ask a blessing from his Heavenly Father,
Becomes a fluent phraseman, absolute
And technical in victories and defeats,
And all our dainty terms for fratricide;
Terms which we trundle smoothly o'er our tongues
Like mere abstractions, empty sounds to which
We join no feeling and attach no form!
As if the soldier died without a wound;
As if the fibres of this godlike frame
Were gored without a pang; as if the wretch,
Who fell in battle, doing bloody deeds,
Passed off to Heaven, translated and not killed;
As though he had no wife to pine for him,
No God to judge him! Therefore, evil days
Are coming on us, O my countrymen!
And what if all-avenging Providence,
Strong and retributive, should make us know
The meaning of our words, force us to feel
The desolation and the agony
Of our fierce doings?

    Spare us yet awhile,
Father and God! O! spare us yet awhile!
Oh! let not English women drag their flight
Fainting beneath the burthen of their babes,
Of the sweet infants, that but yesterday
Laughed at the breast! Sons, brothers, husbands, all
Who ever gazed with fondness on the forms
Which grew up with you round the same fire-side,
And all who ever heard the sabbath-bells
Without the infidel's scorn, make yourselves pure!
Stand forth! be men! repel an impious foe,
Impious and false, a light yet cruel race,
Who laugh away all virtue, mingling mirth
With deeds of murder; and still promising
Freedom, themselves too sensual to be free,
Poison life's amities, and cheat the heart
Of faith and quiet hope, and all that soothes,
And all that lifts the spirit! Stand we forth;
Render them back upon the insulted ocean,
And let them toss as idly on its waves
As the vile sea-weed, which some mountain-blast
Swept from our shores! And oh! may we return

Not with a drunken triumph, but with fear,
Repenting of the wrongs with which we stung
So fierce a foe to frenzy!

                I have told,
O Britons! O my brethren! I have told
Most bitter truth, but without bitterness.
Nor deem my zeal or factious or mistimed;
For never can true courage dwell with them,
Who, playing tricks with conscience, dare not look
At their own vices. We have been too long
Dupes of a deep delusion! Some, belike,
Groaning with restless enmity, expect
All change from change of constituted power;
As if a Government had been a robe,
On which our vice and wretchedness were tagged
Like fancy-points and fringes, with the robe
Pulled off at pleasure. Fondly these attach
A radical causation to a few
Poor drudges of chastising Providence,
Who borrow all their hues and qualities
From our own folly and rank wickedness,
Which gave them birth and nursed them. Others, meanwhile,
Dote with a mad idolatry; and all
Who will not fall before their images,
And yield them worship, they are enemies
Even of their country!

                Such have I been deemed—
But, O dear Britain! O my Mother Isle!
Needs must thou prove a name most dear and holy
To me, a son, a brother, and a friend,
A husband, and a father! who revere
All bonds of natural love, and find them all
Within the limits of thy rocky shores.
O native Britain! O my Mother Isle!
How shouldst thou prove aught else but dear and holy
To me, who from thy lakes and mountain-hills,
Thy clouds, thy quiet dales, thy rocks and seas,
Have drunk in all my intellectual life,
All sweet sensations, all ennobling thoughts,
All adoration of God in nature,
All lovely and all honourable things,
Whatever makes this mortal spirit feel
The joy and greatness of its future being?

There lives nor form nor feeling in my soul
Unborrowed from my country! O divine
And beauteous island! thou hast been my sole
And most magnificent temple, in the which
I walk with awe, and sing my stately songs,
Loving the God that made me!—

                          May my fears,
My filial fears, be vain! and may the vaunts
And menace of the vengeful enemy
Pass like the gust, that roared and died away
In the distant tree: which heard, and only heard
In this low dell, bowed not the delicate grass.

  But now the gentle dew-fall sends abroad
The fruit-like perfume of the golden furze:
The light has left the summit of the hill,
Though still a sunny gleam lies beautiful,
Aslant the ivied beacon. Now farewell,
Farewell, awhile, O soft and silent spot!
On the green sheep-track, up the heathy hill,
Homeward I wind my way; and lo! recalled
From bodings that have well-nigh wearied me,
I find myself upon the brow, and pause
Startled! And after lonely sojourning
In such a quiet and surrounded nook,
This burst of prospect, here the shadowy main,
Dim tinted, there the mighty majesty
Of that huge amphitheatre of rich
And elmy fields, seems like society—
Conversing with the mind, and giving it
A livelier impulse and a dance of thought!
And now, belovéd Stowey! I behold
Thy church-tower, and, methinks, the four huge elms
Clustering, which mark the mansion of my friend;
And close behind them, hidden from my view,
Is my own lowly cottage, where my babe
And my babe's mother dwell in peace! With light
And quickened footsteps thitherward I tend,
Remembering thee, O green and silent dell!
And grateful, that by nature's quietness
And solitary musings, all my heart
Is softened, and made worthy to indulge
Love, and the thoughts that yearn for human kind.

N.B. The above is perhaps not Poetry,—but rather a sort of middle thing between Poetry and Oratory—sermoni propriora.—Some parts are, I am conscious, too tame even for animated prose.

The Nightingale

[1798]

A CONVERSATIONAL POEM, APRIL, 1798.

No cloud, no relique of the sunken day
Distinguishes the West, no long thin slip
Of sullen Light, no obscure trembling hues.
Come, we will rest on this old mossy Bridge!
You see the glimmer of the stream beneath,
But hear no murmuring: it flows silently
O'er its soft bed of verdure. All is still,
A balmy night! and tho' the stars be dim,
Yet let us think upon the vernal showers
That gladden the green earth, and we shall find
A pleasure in the dimness of the stars.
And hark! the Nightingale begins its song,
"Most musical, most melancholy"[60] Bird!
A melancholy Bird? O idle thought!
In nature there is nothing melancholy.
But some night-wandering Man, whose heart was pierced
With the remembrance of a grievous wrong,
Or slow distemper or neglected love,
(And so, poor Wretch! fill'd all things with himself
And made all gentle sounds tell back the tale
Of his own sorrows) he and such as he
First named these notes a melancholy strain;
And many a poet echoes the conceit,
Poet, who hath been building up the rhyme
When he had better far have stretch'd his limbs
Beside a brook in mossy forest-dell
By sun or moonlight, to the influxes
Of shapes and sounds and shifting elements
Surrendering his whole spirit, of his song

---

[60] "Most musical, most melancholy." This passage in Milton possesses an excellence far superior to that of mere description: it is spoken in the character of the melancholy Man, and has therefore a dramatic propriety. The Author makes this remark, to rescue himself from the charge of having alluded with levity to a line of Milton: a charge than which none could be more painful to him, except perhaps that of having ridiculed his Bible.

Samuel Taylor Coleridge

And of his fame forgetful! So his fame
Should share in nature's immortality,
A venerable thing! and so his song
Should make all nature lovelier, and itself
Be lov'd, like nature!—But 'twill not be so;
And youths and maidens most poetical
Who lose the deepening twilights of the spring
In ball-rooms and hot theatres, they still
Full of meek sympathy must heave their sighs
O'er Philomela's pity-pleading strains.

My Friend, and my Friend's Sister! we have learnt
A different lore: we may not thus profane
Nature's sweet voices always full of love
And joyance! 'Tis the merry Nightingale
That crowds, and hurries, and precipitates
With fast thick warble his delicious notes,
As he were fearful, that an April night
Would be too short for him to utter forth
His love-chant, and disburthen his full soul
Of all its music!
              And I know a grove
Of large extent, hard by a castle huge
Which the great lord inhabits not: and so
This grove is wild with tangling underwood,
And the trim walks are broken up, and grass,
Thin grass and king-cups grow within the paths.
But never elsewhere in one place I knew
So many Nightingales: and far and near
In wood and thicket over the wide grove
They answer and provoke each other's songs—
With skirmish and capricious passagings,
And murmurs musical and swift jug jug
And one low piping sound more sweet than all—
Stirring the air with such an harmony,
That should you close your eyes, you might almost
Forget it was not day! On moonlight bushes,
Whose dewy leaflets are but half-disclosed,
You may perchance behold them on the twigs,
Their bright, bright eyes, their eyes both bright and full,
Glistening, while many a glow-worm in the shade
Lights up her love-torch.
                   A most gentle maid
Who dwelleth in her hospitable home
Hard by the Castle, and at latest eve,

(Even like a Lady vowed and dedicate
To something more than nature in the grove)
Glides thro' the pathways; she knows all their notes,
That gentle Maid! and oft, a moment's space,
What time the moon was lost behind a cloud,
Hath heard a pause of silence: till the Moon
Emerging, hath awakened earth and sky
With one sensation, and those wakeful Birds
Have all burst forth in choral minstrelsy,
As if one quick and sudden Gale had swept
An hundred airy harps! And she hath watch'd
Many a Nightingale perch giddily
On blossomy twig still swinging from the breeze,
And to that motion tune his wanton song,
Like tipsy Joy that reels with tossing head.

Farewell, O Warbler! till to-morrow eve,
And you, my friends! farewell, a short farewell!
We have been loitering long and pleasantly,
And now for our dear homes.—That strain again!
Full fain would it delay me!—My dear Babe,
Who, capable of no articulate sound,
Mars all things with his imitative lisp,
How he would place his hand beside his ear,
His little hand, the small forefinger up,
And bid us listen! And I deem it wise
To make him Nature's playmate. He knows well
The evening star: and once when he awoke
In most distressful mood (some inward pain
Had made up that strange thing, an infant's dream)
I hurried with him to our orchard plot,
And he beholds the moon, and hush'd at once
Suspends his sobs, and laughs most silently,
While his fair eyes that swam with undropped tears
Did glitter in the yellow moon-beam! Well—
It is a father's tale. But if that Heaven
Should give me life, his childhood shall grow up
Familiar with these songs, that with the night
He may associate Joy! Once more farewell,
Sweet Nightingale! once more, my friends! farewell.

Dejection: An Ode

[1802]

> Late, late yestreen I saw the new Moon,
> With the old Moon in her arms;
> And I fear, I fear, my Master dear!
> We shall have a deadly storm.
> Ballad of Sir Patrick Spence.

I

Well! If the Bard was weather-wise, who made
   The grand old ballad of Sir Patrick Spence,
   This night, so tranquil now, will not go hence
Unroused by winds, that ply a busier trade
Than those which mould yon cloud in lazy flakes,
Or the dull sobbing drafty that moans and rakes
Upon the strings of this Æolian lute,
      Which better far were mute.
   For lo! the New-moon winter-bright!
   And overspread with phantom light,
    (With swimming phantom light o'erspread
    But rimmed and circled by a silver thread)
I see the old Moon in her lap, foretelling
   The, coming-on of rain and squally blast.
And oh that even now the gust were swelling,
   And the slant night-shower driving loud and fast!
Those sounds which oft have raised me, whilst they awed,
     And sent my soul abroad,
Might now perhaps their wonted impulse give,
Might startle this dull pain, and make it move and live!

II

A grief without a pang, void, dark, and drear,
   A stifled, drowsy, unimpassioned grief,
   Which finds no natural outlet, no relief,
      In word, or sigh, or tear—
O Lady! in this wan and heartless mood,
To other thoughts by yonder throstle woo'd,
   All this long eve, so balmy and serene,
Have I been gazing on the western sky,
   And its peculiar tint of yellow green:

And still I gaze—and with how blank an eye
And those thin clouds above, in flakes and bars,
That give away their motion to the stars;
Those stars, that glide behind them or between,
Now sparkling, now bedimmed, but always seen
Yon crescent Moon, as fixed as if it grew
In its own cloudless, starless lake of blue;
I see them all so excellently fair,
I see, not feel, how beautiful they are!

III

    My genial spirits fail;
    And what can these avail
To lift the smothering weight from off my breast?
    It were a vain endeavour,
    Though I should gaze for ever
On that green light that lingers in the west:
I may not hope from outward forms to win
The passion and the life, whose fountains are within.

IV

O Lady! we receive but what we give,
And in our life alone does Nature live:
Ours is her wedding-garment, ours her shroud!
    And would we aught behold, of higher worth,
Than that inanimate cold world allowed
To the poor loveless, ever-anxious crowd,
    Ah! from the soul itself must issue forth
A light, a glory, a fair luminous cloud—
    Enveloping the Earth—
And from the soul itself must there be sent
    A sweet and potent voice, of its own birth,
Of all sweet sounds the life and element!

V

O pure of heart! thou need'st not ask of me
What this strong music in the soul may be!
What, and wherein it doth exist,
This light, this glory, this fair luminous mist,
This beautiful and beauty-making power.
    Joy, virtuous Lady! Joy that ne'er was given,
Save to the pure, and in their purest hour,

Life, and Life's effluence, cloud at once and shower,
Joy, Lady! is the spirit and the power,
Which wedding Nature to us gives in dower,
   A new Earth and new Heaven,
Undreamt of by the sensual and the proud—
Joy is the sweet voice, Joy the luminous cloud—
   We in ourselves rejoice!
And thence flows all that charms or ear or sight,
   All melodies the echoes of that voice,
All colours a suffusion from that light.

VI

There was a time when, though my path was rough,
   This joy within me dallied with distress,
And all misfortunes were but as the stuff
   Whence Fancy made me dreams of happiness:
For hope grew round me, like the twining vine,
And fruits, and foliage, not my own, seemed mine.
But now afflictions bow me down to earth:
Nor care I that they rob me of my mirth
   But oh! each visitation
Suspends what nature gave me at my birth,
   My shaping spirit of Imagination.
For not to think of what I needs must feel,
   But to be still and patient, all I can;
And haply by abstruse research to steal
   From my own nature all the natural man—
   This was my sole resource, my only plan:
Till that which suits a part infects the whole,
And now is almost grown the habit of my soul.

VII

Hence, viper thoughts, that coil around my mind,
    Reality's dark dream!
I turn from you, and listen to the wind,
   Which long has raved unnoticed. What a scream
Of agony by torture lengthened out
   That lute sent forth! Thou Wind, that rav'st without,
   Bare crag, or mountain-tairn, or blasted tree,
Or pine-grove whither woodman never clomb,
Or lonely house, long held the witches' home,
   Methinks were fitter instruments for thee,
Mad Lutanist! who in this month of showers,

Of dark-brown gardens, and of peeping flowers,
Mak'st Devils' yule, with worse than wintry song,
The blossoms, buds, and timorous leaves among.
   Thou Actor, perfect in all tragic sounds!
Thou mighty Poet, even to frenzy bold!
      What tell'st thou now about?
     'Tis of the rushing of an host in rout,
  With groans of trampled men, with smarting wounds—
At once they groan with pain, and shudder with the cold!
But hush! there is a pause of deepest silence!
  And all that noise, as of a rushing crowd,
With groans, and tremulous shudderings-all is over—
   It tells another tale, with sounds less deep and loud!
     A tale of less affright,
     And tempered with delight,
As Otway's self had framed the tender lay,
      'Tis of a little child
      Upon a lonesome wild,
Not far from home, but she hath lost her way:
And now moans low in bitter grief and fear,
And now screams loud, and hopes to make her mother hear.

VIII

Tis midnight, but small thoughts have I of sleep:
Full seldom may my friend such vigils keep!
Visit her, gentle Sleep! with wings of healing,
  And may this storm be but a mountain-birth,
May all the stars hang bright above her dwelling,
  Silent as though they watched the sleeping Earth!
     With light heart may she rise,
     Gay fancy, cheerful eyes,
  Joy lift her spirit, joy attune her voice;
To her may all things live, from pole to pole,
Their life the eddying of her living soul!
  O simple spirit, guided from above,
Dear Lady! friend devoutest of my choice,
Thus mayest thou ever, evermore rejoice.

The Pains of Sleep

[1803]

Ere on my bed my limbs I lay,
It hath not been my use to pray
With moving lips or bended knees;
But silently, by slow degrees,
My spirit I to Love compose,
In humble trust mine eye-lids close,
With reverential resignation,
No wish conceived, no thought exprest,
Only a *sense* of supplication;
A sense o'er all my soul imprest
That I am weak, yet not unblest,
Since in me, round me, everywhere
Eternal Strength and Wisdom are.

But yester-night I prayed aloud
In anguish and in agony,
Up-starting from the fiendish crowd
Of shapes and thoughts that tortured me:
A lurid light, a trampling throng,
Sense of intolerable wrong,
And whom I scorned, those only strong!
Thirst of revenge, the powerless will
Still baffled, and yet burning still!
Desire with loathing strangely mixed
On wild or hateful objects fixed.
Fantastic passions! maddening brawl!
And shame and terror over all!
Deeds to be hid which were not hid,
Which all confused I could not know
Whether I suffered, or I did:
For all seem'd guilt, remorse or woe,
My own or others still the same
Life-stifling fear, soul-stifling shame!

So two nights passed: the night's dismay
Saddened and stunned the coming day.
Sleep, the wide blessing, seemed to me
Distemper's worst calamity.
The third night, when my own loud scream
Had waked me from the fiendish dream,

O'ercome with sufferings strange and wild,
I wept as I had been a child;
And having thus by tears subdued
My anguish to a milder mood,
Such punishments, I said, were due
To natures deepliest stained with sin:
For aye entempesting anew
The unfathomable hell within
The horror of their deeds to view,
To know and loathe, yet wish and do!
Such griefs with such men well agree,
But wherefore, wherefore fall on me?
To be beloved is all I need,
And whom I love, I love indeed.

To William Wordsworth

[1807]

COMPOSED ON THE NIGHT AFTER HIS RECITATION OF A
POEM ON THE GROWTH OF AN INDIVIDUAL MIND

Friend of the Wise! and Teacher of the Good!
Into my heart have I received that Lay
More than historic, that prophetic Lay
Wherein (high theme by thee first sung aright)
Of the foundations and the building up
Of a Human Spirit thou hast dared to tell
What may be told, to the understanding mind
Revealable; and what within the mind
By vital breathings secret as the soul
Of vernal growth, oft quickens in the heart
Thoughts all too deep for words!—

                        Theme hard as high!
Of smiles spontaneous, and mysterious fears
(The first-born they of Reason and twin-birth),
Of tides obedient to external force,
And currents self-determined, as might seem,
Or by some inner Power; of moments awful,
Now in thy inner life, and now abroad,
When power streamed from thee, and thy soul received
The light reflected, as a light bestowed—
Of fancies fair, and milder hours of youth,
Hyblean murmurs of poetic thought

Industrious in its joy, in vales and glens
Native or outland, lakes and famous hills!
Or on the lonely high-road, when the stars
Were rising; or by secret mountain-streams,
The guides and the companions of thy way!

Of more than Fancy, of the Social Sense
Distending wide, and man beloved as man,
Where France in all her towns lay vibrating
Like some becalmèd bark beneath the burst
Of Heaven's immediate thunder, when no cloud
Is visible, or shadow on the main.
For thou wert there, thine own brows garlanded,
Amid the tremor of a realm aglow,
Amid the mighty nation jubilant,
When from the general heart of human kind
Hope sprang forth like a full-born Diety!
—Of that dear Hope afflicted and struck down,
So summoned homeward, thenceforth calm and sure
From the dread watch-tower of man's absolute self,
With light unwaning on her eyes, to look
Far on—herself a glory to behold,
The Angel of the vision! Then (last strain)
Of Duty, chosen Laws controlling choice,
Action and Joy!—An Orphic song indeed,
A song divine of high and passionate thoughts
To their own music chaunted!

                        O great Bard!
Ere yet that last strain dying awed the air,
With stedfast eye I viewed thee in the choir
Of ever-enduring men. The truly great
Have all one age, and from one visible space
Shed influence! They, both in power and act,
Are permanent, and Time is not with them,
Save as it worketh for them, they in it.
Nor less a sacred Roll, than those of old,
And to be placed, as they, with gradual fame
Among the archives of mankind, thy work
Makes audible a linkèd lay of Truth,
Of Truth profound a sweet continuous lay,
Not learnt, but native, her own natural notes!
Ah! as I listened with a heart forlorn,
The pulses of my being beat anew:
And even as Life returns upon the drowned,

Life's joy rekindling roused a throng of pains—
Keen pangs of Love, awakening as a babe
Turbulent, with an outcry in the heart;
And Fears self-willed, that shunned the eye of Hope;
And Hope that scarce would know itself from Fear;
Sense of past Youth, and Manhood come in vain,
And Genius given, and Knowledge won in vain;
And all which I had culled in wood-walks wild,
And all which patient toil had reared, and all,
Commune with thee had opened out—but flowers
Strewed on my corse, and borne upon my bier,
In the same coffin, for the self-same grave!

    That way no more! and ill beseems it me,
Who came a welcomer in herald's guise,
Singing of Glory, and Futurity,
To wander back on such unhealthful road,
Plucking the poisons of self-harm! And ill
Such intertwine beseems triumphal wreaths
Strew'd before thy advancing!

                    Nor do thou,
Sage Bard! impair the memory of that hour
Of thy communion with my nobler mind
By pity or grief, already felt too long!
Nor let my words import more blame than needs.
The tumult rose and ceased: for Peace is nigh
Where Wisdom's voice has found a listening heart.
Amid the howl of more than wintry storms,
The Halcyon hears the voice of vernal hours
Already on the wing.

                Eve following eve,
Dear tranquil time, when the sweet sense of Home
Is sweetest! moments for their own sake hailed
And more desired, more precious, for thy song,
In silence listening, like a devout child,
My soul lay passive, by thy various strain
Driven as in surges now beneath the stars,
With momentary stars of my own birth,
Fair constellated foam, still darting off
Into the darkness; now a tranquil sea,
Outspread and bright, yet swelling to the moon.
And when—O Friend! my comforter and guide!
Strong in thyself, and powerful to give strength!—

Thy long sustainéd Song finally closed,
And thy deep voice had ceased—yet thou thyself
Wert still before my eyes, and round us both
That happy vision of belovéd faces—
Scarce conscious, and yet conscious of its close
I sate, my being blended in one thought
(Thought was it? or aspiration? or resolve?)
Absorbed, yet hanging still upon the sound—
And when I rose, I found myself in prayer.

THE END

www.ingramcontent.com/pod-product-compliance
Lightning Source LLC
Chambersburg PA
CBHW031411040426
42444CB00005B/513